# An Agrarian Proposal

# An Agrarian Proposal

New England Agrarianism in Service of the
Common Good

Rebecca Judge *and*
Charles Taliaferro

CASCADE *Books* · Eugene, Oregon

AN AGRARIAN PROPOSAL
New England Agrarianism in Service of the Common Good

Cascade Books
An Imprint of Wipf and Stock Publishers
199 W. 8th Ave., Suite 3
Eugene, OR 97401

www.wipfandstock.com

PAPERBACK ISBN: 978-1-6667-1009-0
HARDCOVER ISBN: 978-1-6667-1010-6
EBOOK ISBN: 978-1-6667-1011-3

*Cataloguing-in-Publication data:*

Names: Judge, Rebecca [author]. | Taliaferro, Charles [author]

Title: An agrarian proposal : New England agrarianism in service of the common good / Rebecca Judge and Charles Taliaferro.

Description: Eugene, OR: Cascade Books, 2022 | Includes bibliographical references and index.

Identifiers: ISBN 978-1-6667-1009-0 (paperback) | ISBN 978-1-6667-1010-6 (hardcover) | ISBN 978-1-6667-1011-3 (ebook)

Subjects: LCSH: Human ecology—New England—History | New England—History | Agriculture—Moral and ethical aspects | Agriculture—Environmental aspects | Agriculture—Economic aspects | Agriculture—Religious aspects—Christianity

Classification: GF504.N45 J83 2022 (print) | GF504.N45 (ebook)

11/30/22

# Contents

# Acknowledgements

WE WISH TO EXPRESS our immense gratitude to our editor, Revd. Dr. Robin Parry, whose encouragement and close reading of our work was truly inspirational.

We also acknowledge with thanksgiving colleagues, friends, and family who supported us, inspired us, and tolerated us as we labored on this project. Among these are Gene Bakko, who changed Taliaferro's life as a gifted co-teacher of a course on the ethics and biology of agriculture. Other faculty colleagues who have inspired both of us by their interest in reclaiming agriculture as a calling include Ed Langerak, DeAne Lagerquist, Kathy Shea, Charles Umbanhower, and Charles Wilson. We are also grateful for the contributions of Garry Comstock, David Legvold, and Rick Taylor.

Finally, we thank our colleagues and spouses, Anthony Becker and Jil Evans, for their wise insights and faithful encouragement.

# Introduction

FROM A WORLD HISTORICAL perspective, the birth of agriculture some ten thousand years ago marks a major shift in human history; without surplus agriculture there could be no cities or standing armies. Productive agriculture, sustained by irrigation, tools, and domesticated animals, has served as the foundation for almost every stage of human history in terms of the development of communities, households, languages, transportation, political and economic life, religion, military power, trade, and the evolution of law and its institutions of discipline, punishment, and the distribution of benefits and liabilities. Conversely, the collapse of agriculture in a region, both historically and today, is invariably a crisis for persons and domesticated nonhuman animals, the site of die-outs, compulsory migration, and other traumatic events. Despite the indisputable importance of agriculture, farming has not always been praised as a vital, virtuous practice.

*Agrarianism* is the term used today to identify the philosophy and practice of farming that does not praise any and all farming, but valorizes farming when it is an important cultural site for the cultivation of virtue, both in terms of civic life and in terms of the sustained stewardship of land and animals. There is a long history of praising farming as a special vocation that can be traced back to Greco-Roman times in the work of Cato, Virgil, Seneca, Cicero, and Horace, among others. While Plato did not elevate farming as a practice for the rulers of his ideal city (the Republic), he recognized that his city required the service of lifelong, productive, reliable farmers. Aristotle identified the household, including the farm household, as the foundation of the city or *polis*. While farming has been viewed as just another form of production (farmers are involved in food production while a mason is involved in producing stone buildings), those recognized as agrarians see good farming—often small-scale as opposed to large, corporate, market-driven farming—as a complex set of inter-related goods: the proper care of land and animals, good neighborly, community-oriented practices, intergenerational cooperation, self-sufficiency, and more.

Throughout most of its existence, agrarianism has been associated with the just, or equal, distribution of the land as a means of sustenance. The word, *agrarian,* itself goes back to Roman times, when the *lex agrarian,* or agrarian laws, governed the appropriation of cultivated land acquired through Roman conquest. Some of these lands became the *ager publicus,* or public lands, so designated with the intent of providing a supply of cultivated land for the poor by limiting the amount of conquered lands that any single citizen could lay claim to, even via otherwise legal market transactions. Centuries later, eighteenth-century philosopher James Harrington, in his *The Commonwealth of Oceana,* described agrarian law as that which concerns "fixing the balance in lands." Of their origins, Harrington argues that agrarian laws were "first introduced by God himself, who divided the land of Canaan to his people by lots." Harrington appears to be referring to passages in Joshua that describe God's direct involvement in land allocation among the twelve tribes in the soon-to-be occupied lands of Canaan (Josh 14:2 and 18:1–10). This balance in lands was essential, according to Harrington, as without it, "government, whether monarchical, aristocratical, or popular, has no long lease."[1] While

---

1. Harrington, *The Commonwealth of Oceana,* 12.

Harrington only spoke of *balance* in the distribution of land, by the end of the eighteenth century, agrarianism was associated with the "forced equalization of the ownership of cultivated land."[2] As such, it was an anathema among the liberty-loving founders of this nation. Thomas Jefferson himself praised the American Congress for providing "protection against the agrarian and plundering enterprises of the majority of the people."[3]

Over time, however, and largely through the influence of the Twelve Southerners, the term has taken on an entirely different meaning.[4] "The theory of agrarianism," according to these writers, "is that the culture of the soil is the best and most sensitive of vocations, and that therefore it should have the economic preferences."[5] From this perspective, agrarianism is often seen as reaching a highpoint in Thomas Jefferson's 1781 "Notes on the State of Virginia."

It has to be said at the outset that while Jefferson's agrarianism may have admirable aspects, the man was deeply embedded in the racism of his day. Still, we cite him below at length because Jefferson articulates some of the seminal ideals of an agrarianism that persists today. Those ideals include his recognition of the value of the farmer in the life of a democratic culture (some agrarians today advocate what they call "food democracy"), his view of the importance of farmers being self-sufficient, free of the corruption that seems rife in cities, and specifically his contrast between the virtues of a farmer and the vices of an industrialist.

Jefferson writes:

2. Govan, "Agrarian and Agrarianism," 36.

3. Jefferson, quoted in Saul K. Padover (ed.), *The Complete Jefferson*, 283.

4. The "Twelve Southerners" was the name taken by a group of (twelve) writers associated with Vanderbilt University who in 1930 jointly authored *Ill Take My Stand*, a collection of essays promoting a particular, somewhat romantic vision of the southern United States and its culture. The group included Donald Davison, John Gould Fletcher, Henry Blue Kline, Lyle Lanier, Andrew Nelson Lytle, Herman Clarence Nixon, Frank Lawrence Owsley, John Crowe Ranson, Allen Tate, John Donald Wade, Robert Penn Warren, and Stark Young.

5. Twelve Southerners, *I'll Take My Stand*, li.

Those who labour in the earth are the chosen people of God, if ever he had a chosen people, whose breasts he has made his peculiar deposit for substantial and genuine virtue. It is the focus in which he keeps alive that sacred fire, which otherwise might escape from the face of the earth. Corruption of morals in the mass of cultivators is a phenomenon of which no age nor nation has furnished an example. It is the mark set on those, who not looking up to heaven, to their own soil and industry, as does the husbandman, for their subsistence, depend for it on the casualties and caprice of customers. Dependence begets subservience and venality, suffocates the germ of virtue, and prepares fit tools for the designs of ambition. This, the natural progress and consequence of the arts, has sometimes perhaps been retarded by accidental circumstances: but, generally speaking, the proportion which the aggregate of the other classes of citizens bears in any state to that of its husbandmen, is the proportion of its unsound to its healthy parts, and is a good-enough barometer whereby to measure its degree of corruption. While we have land to labour then, let us never wish to see our citizens occupied at a work-bench, or twirling a distaff. Carpenters, masons, smiths, are wanting in husbandry: but, for the general operations of manufacture, let our work-shops remain in Europe.[6]

As noted, Jefferson was hardly consistent in many areas. While he spoke favorably of limited federal governance, he held three national offices, including the presidency, and expanded the size of the United States dramatically with the Louisiana Purchase. In any case, Jefferson's spirited form of agrarianism had some influence on the Twelve Southerners and their intellectual heirs. Especially relevant for those agrarians in the southern United States was a suspicion of big government's impact on farming. A contemporary of Jefferson's, John Taylor, writing in 1814 does "not recall a

---

6. Jefferson's "Notes on the State of Virginia," online: https://www.pbs.org/wgbh/aia/part3/3h490t.html. Accessed 9/25/21.

single law, state or continental, passed in favor of agriculture" and blames government of the wretched state of farmers.[7]

Agrarianism today is represented by individuals who, for the most part, follow Jefferson's understanding of farming as a source of virtue. Wendell Berry, James Hightower, Wes Jackson, Frederick Krishenmann, Paul Thompson, and other vibrant advocates of healthy farm communities support farmers, even as they are careful to avoid endorsing government regulation of farming practices. Some of these agrarians are professing Christians who completely undermine the prejudice often found among environmental advocates and philosophers working in environmental ethics that Christianity offers its full support to an ethic of human superiority to, and the domination over, all other forms of life (Lynn White, Paul Taylor, Roderick Nash, J. B. Callicott, and so on). Christianity has been ably defended against this charge by philosophers who stress the Christian tradition of stewardship (Robin Attfield, Holmes Rolston III), but a reply seems all the more compelling when a practicing Christian farmer such as Wendell Berry demonstrates in his life the interwoven nature of healthy spirituality and good land stewardship. Not all American agrarians are Christians, of course; Thomas Jefferson's Christianity was more deistic than theistic (no miracles, special revelation, or incarnation) and some leading agrarians today, such as Paul Thompson, are secular.

The agrarianism of Wendell Berry has been widely praised. On our own campus at St. Olaf College, in Northfield, Minnesota, students and faculty have often organized an honor house for fourth year (senior) students who desire to dedicate themselves to Berry's holistic vision of life in community. Here is the mission statement of this honor house:

> The mission of the Wendell Berry House is to reestablish the link between people, communities, and the food that we eat. We strive to promote the idea that a sustainable life means sustaining not only Mother Earth, but also the body, the mind, and the community of which each individual is a part. Throughout the year we will be hosting

7. John Taylor, *Arator*, 421–42.

events and lessons that aim to give students the everyday tools they need to live as ecological citizens of our beautiful planet. We will be teaming up with other student organizations to host different events (all of which will involve delicious local food).[8]

The House cites this passage from Berry's work that is admirable and revealing.

A community is the mental and spiritual condition of knowing that the place is shared, and that the people who share the place define and limit the possibilities of each other's lives. It is the knowledge that people have of each other, their concern for each other, their trust in each other, the freedom with which they come and go among themselves.[9]

As we noted, Berry is much admired, but we do have some serious reservations about Berry and the tradition of Jeffersonian agrarian individualism and its negative view of government. Note that in the above cited passage, Berry stresses "the freedom with which they come and go among themselves." From time to time, Berry takes a conspiratorial view of government, arguing that it works "to guarantee the right of the most wealthy to own or control the land without limit."[10] Kirshenmann similarly laments the failure of government when it comes to farming, arguing that—billions of farm subsidies notwithstanding—"farmers have no one to champion their cause."[11]

Our book, *An Agrarian Proposal*, advocates agrarianism, but our proposal is that *we should learn from, and be inspired by agrarianism as practiced by New England's first European settlers.* The early New Englanders promoted a practical communitarianism, as expressed in their political and religious institutions, in which the

---

8. St. Olaf website: https://sustainabilities.stolaf.edu/wendell-berry-house/. Accessed 9/25/21.

9. Wendell Berry: https://quotepark.com/quotes/2068636-wendell-berry-a-community-is-the-mental-and-spiritual-condition/. Accessed: 9/25/21.

10. Berry, "The Agrarian Standard," 29.

11. Kirshenmann, *Cultivating an Ecological Conscience*, 23.

good of the whole was paramount. For at least a century after their hard-scrapple beginnings at Plymouth, New England settlers faced a physical reality that compelled them to promote the good of the whole, even as their theology emphasized a mandate for mutual love and forbearance. Our current physical realities, as reflected in climate change, resource depletion, and species' extinction argue in favor of restoring the commons as an organizing principle and a physical reality. For two centuries, we have privileged the individualism celebrated by agrarians as informed by Jefferson. We argue that it is time to reconsider the modest, quieter, less-charismatic, and less individualistic agrarianism realized in colonial New England.

We are not the only ones to have reservations about the ideals of Jeffersonian agrarianism. The anti-government sentiments of this school of thought have been recognized by some as contributing to the unfortunate schism that exists to this day between environmentalists and those engaged in farming. Environmentalists long ago learned to rely on, or at least partner with, government to achieve their goals, while many agrarians, following Jefferson's lead, continue to chafe at government's bit. Although some have attempted to explain away the jarring incongruence between the Jeffersonian agrarian portrait of the virtuous farmer and the massive environmental harm wreaked by agriculture by blaming exogenous factors, or by asserting that farmers are simply "oblivious to the accumulative effects of many farms,"[12] we propose that the Jeffersonian agrarian narrative has protected agricultural producers from government by associating the unconstrained liberty-loving farmer with virtue. It has also disadvantaged would-be practitioners of an ethical agrarianism by forcing them to compete, as if on a level playing field, against members of their profession whose only interest in farming is its contribution to the bottom line.

The excesses of unregulated agricultural practices convince us that, if agriculture is to regain its agrarian footing and reflect a decent and virtuous commitment to humanity and the earth that supports us, agrarians need to develop ways to work with

12. Thompson, *The Spirit of the Soil,* 86.

government at the international, national, state, and county levels, to develop a policy regime that coordinates agricultural production and processes with social, humane, and ecological goals. We propose that the development of this agrarian regulatory policy agenda might be profitably enhanced by an examination of the agrarian tradition found in colonial New England, a tradition that privileges the care of the land and the just distribution of its bounty over concern for the individual who farms it.

Our work is informed not only by an historical description of the New England agrarian tradition as reflected in land use and land ownership practices in colonial New England, but by a careful study of the philosophical and theological commitments that gave rise to colonial New England's agrarianism, particularly as expressed through the institution of the commons. This study is the focus of chapter 1. As the commons represents the most salient material expression of New England's agrarianism, we devote chapter 2 to an examination of the land use practices, the regulatory processes, and the regulatory constraints that were employed to maintain the land-based commons as a means of providing a sustainable means of sustenance to New England settlers. Chapter 3 traces how, beginning in the second half of the eighteenth century, an ever-increasing emphasis on individual freedom and liberty, coupled with the ever-expanding U.S. frontier, eventually eroded political support for New England's regulatory-intensive, individually constraining communitarian-based agrarianism, and brought about its demise. We conclude our book in chapter 4 with an examination of steps we might take to reclaim a land-based, communitarian agrarian ethos that successfully and sustainably supported New England's colonial settlers for two hundred years.

Chapter One

------------

# An Agrarian Integration in the New England Colonies

"The free fruition of such liberties Immunities and priveledges as humanitie, Civilitie, and Christianitie call for as due to every man in his place and proportion without impeachment and Infringement hath ever bene and ever will be the tranquillitie and Stabilitie of Churches and Commonwealths."[1]

—Massachusetts Body of Liberties (1641)

HISTORIANS AGREE THAT THE Body of Liberties was the first legal code adopted in New England by European colonists. But they disagree about its actual impact on the General Court, the General Laws of Massachusetts, and the Bill of Rights. Similarly, many or most historians acknowledge an early agrarian ideal among the British colonists. The American agricultural historian, Douglas Hurt offers the following sketch of the agrarian ideal:

------------

1. Found online: https://history.hanover.edu/texts/masslib.html. 9/25/21.

> Agrarianism is the belief that farming is the best way of life and the most important economic endeavor. Agrarianism also implies that farmers willfully sought to avoid commercial agriculture and preferred a "moral economy" in which they produced for subsistence purposes rather than the market and economic gain. The agrarian tradition has long been recognized as central to the American experience.[2]

Hurt believes that no such agrarianism ever occurred: "Although the belief in the agrarian tradition remains, it is colored with myth. It paints a mental image of a past that never was while denying the reality of contemporary agricultural life. Agrarianism now, as in the past, remains more myth than reality."[3]

Although we too are suspicious of idealized portraits of agrarianism, we do not share Hurt's dismissal of agrarianism as mythic. Sure, when colonial farmers (north and south) were not principally driven by the fear of starvation, profit functioned as a motive for many, especially for large plantation owners. But we argue in this chapter and the next that there was also farming, especially in New England, that was oriented to the common good and shared responsibility for each others' welfare, which was conceived of in irreducibly religious terms. Thus, we make a case for the centrality of the philosophical and theological frameworks that informed the agricultural practices of the colonies, particularly through their persistent emphasis on the commons according to which agriculture was itself understood to be part of a vocational calling to stewardship of the earth and its resources.

## Colonial Theology on Land and Labor

A foundational concern of the earliest British colonial settlements was a preoccupation with bare survival. Nevertheless, this struggle never overshadowed religious and political reflection; rather, it underscored its importance. The colonists urgently needed a

2. Hurt, *American Agriculture*, 74.
3. Hurt, *American Agriculture*, 73–74.

reliable theological, political, and economic framework that could withstand hardships ranging from epidemics to crop failures to conflicts with Native Americans. As European agricultural practices and land-related property rights translated poorly to life in North America, colonists were forced to adapt, and this led to the development of a new theology of human nature, language, and culture. Forced to incorporate Native American (and thus, at the time, non-Christian) practices of raising crops and to rely on Indian stores of food in crises, the colonists required the guidance of a framework that could ensure that bare economic exchange and agriculture would remain intelligible and feasible. It was this new context that established theology, economic regulation, and politics as practical activities of the colonies.

The Puritans migrating to New England articulated their motivations as a desire to live with integrity both in their relationships with God and with one another. Puritan sermons, journals, and papers from the period commonly highlight the necessity of integrating proper living and right habitation. Failure to live righteously in a land was failure to earn the right to govern in a land. Many Puritans saw the hypocrisy and abuses of power and economic privilege in the Old World as evidence of the illegitimacy of the prevailing church and state. In Great Britain, Puritans and other nonconformists and dissenters opposed episcopacy in the 1630s. By the 1640s, they opposed not only the Church of England (in the person of Bishop Laud), but also the rule of King Charles I. The rapidly unfolding events in this decade dramatically confirmed to the Puritans the political illegitimacy and instability of the government in Britain: the Church of England was abolished in 1644 and Charles I was executed in 1649, the same year that parliament came out in support of the Puritan settlements in New England. Cromwell was made lord protector in 1653, but within seven years he was dead, the monarchy restored, and the Church of England reestablished. The colonists did not universally support Cromwell, and serious colonial support for both Charles I and the restoration did exist all along. Still, the Puritan theology of state and history held that legitimate rule required justice and

3

righteousness. The emphasis placed on the intertwining of right living, right habitation, and government is especially clear in the works of Puritans who opposed both church and crown. Examples include Thomas Hooker's (1586–1647) *The Danger of Desertion*, and John Davenport's (1597–1670) *The Saint's Anchor-Hold*. Davenport upheld the right to hide and protect those who fled Britain at the Restoration in order to escape prosecution on the grounds that a morally corrupt power has no right to prosecute those who oppose it. As John Winthrop described, even in 1629, Europe was hopelessly condemned, as "all other churches of Europe are brought to desolation."[4] He believed that people had lost their commitment to the wellbeing of land and community, it was not widely believed that individual persons should be valued and loved:

> This land grows weary of her inhabitants, so as man who is the most precious of all creatures is here more vile and base than the earth we tread upon, and of less price among us than a horse or a sheep . . . and thus it is come to pass that children, servants and neighbors (especially if the[y] be poor) are counted the greatest burthen, which, if things were right, it would be the chiefest earthly blessing.[5]

Setting themselves against the corruption, sin, and utter lack of community that many colonists believed they were leaving behind, the colonists sought to start a community in which they could be governed by just government and live in right relationship to God and each other. Certainly, there is a significant spiritual element to Winthrop's criticisms of England, but a strong critique of institutions that systematically devalue the poor is also present. Thus, the social and material elements of the commons, which provided for the just distribution of goods and care for the poor and children, were also essential parts of Winthrop's vision of the colonies. Only when individuals—and by extension, communities—not merely feared God but demonstrated love of the

4. Winthrop, *Winthrop's Journal*, "History of New England," *1630–1649*, 239.

5. Winthrop, "A Declaration in Defense of an Order of Court in May 1637," 164.

neighbor in works of mercy did they act in accordance with God's moral law. A large part of the earliest American Puritan teaching was in the great tradition that was forged in the European Reformation on the basis of biblical narratives and teaching. According to this tradition, human beings are related to God in a twofold fashion, first by creation and then by regeneration. The appeal to creation is foundational and deserves the lengthier treatment here, for the philosophy of creation had a vital role in colonial reflection on land and labor. According to the Christian theism of the seventeenth- and eighteenth-century British colonies, God is the supreme Creator of the cosmos. In contrast to our contingent and temporal world, God exists necessarily and eternally. This God is omnipotent, omniscient, omnipresent, and all-good. The dependence of the cosmos upon God is radical; it is no more possible for such a world to outgrow its dependence upon God than that it is for a number to be so great that no greater number exists. On this model, the existence of the cosmos at any given moment is fundamentally, but not exhaustively, constituted by God's creativity (not exhaustively because of free will of creatures). Thus, our very being is derived from God, and any powers we possess are due to the generosity, creativity, and sustained will of the all-good Creator. Some American theologians disagreed about whether God sustains the same world by a continuous creative act, or continually re-creates it at each point in its existence (implying that the cosmos is successively created out of nothing at each instant). Either way, the cosmos is so profoundly dependent upon God that were God's creative power to be withdrawn, the cosmos would cease to exist. The dependence of the cosmos upon the creativity of this God had dramatic ethical, economic, and political implications. It placed within God a supreme power and implied that the whole cosmos belongs to God. In this overarching theology, we humans are God's; indeed, the *entirety of the cosmos is considered God's property*. Thus, the cosmos is delineated as something that is owned. Rather than something radically evil or alien to omnibenevolence, wisdom, and virtue, this cosmos is instead the creation of the being whose omnibenevolence, wisdom, and perfection are unsurpassed. Property rights, therefore, are not invented by humans; rather, they originate with God. In this regard, New England theology largely remained in line with greater Christianity, in addition to Judaism and Islam.

In *God's Promise to His Plantations*, John Cotton (1585–1652) lays out a strong version of the thesis that all of creation belongs to God. Because of God's supreme authority as Creator of all things, including land, God may give land to those whom God chooses: "This placing of people in this or that country is from God's sovereignty over all the earth, and the inhabitants thereof, as in Psalms 24:1, The Earth is the Lord's, and the fullness thereof. Therefore it is meet he should provide a place for all nations to inhabit, and have all the earth replenished."[6] Cotton's appeal to scriptural authority certainly matches the reformed readings of early biblical narratives, which frequently appeared in covenantal, colonial sermons. The most common biblical stories appealed to were the divine promise and guidance offered to Abraham (Gen 15 and 17), to Noah (Gen 8–17), to Moses and the Israelites in their exodus from slavery in Egypt and their journey to the promise land (first six books of the Bible), and to the disciples of Christ in the new covenant (e.g., Luke 22:20). Of course, divine authority and entitlement has often been cited to justify ends that include oppressive monarchies, feudalism, slavery, animal mistreatment, and genocides of native populations. In the beginning, however, colonists appealed to divine ownership primarily as a way to establish *a commons*, an area to be viewed as belonging to the group rather than an individual. As part of his bounteous gift to people during creation, many believed God gave land to both individuals and groups (for example, parishes) in virtue of their promise to cultivate the land and flourish. In concurrence with typical colonial theology, humans were believed to be created in God's image. Thus, the colonists thought persons have God-given powers that, when used properly, could contribute to their personal welfare, the welfare of others, and to the glory of God. To exercise one's

6. Cotton, "God's Promise to His Plantations," 77. See also Ezek 18:4, 1 Chr 29:11–19.

powers towards cultivation and improvement of something in the commons was to come to take possession of it in a way that protected it from the use of others. While this human power was on a very different footing than God's power in creation, rightful human endeavor may still be seen as a reflection of God's abundant creativity. This understanding of the origin of property rights was often conveyed with biblical examples and held in check by appeal to biblical teaching. Thus, the right to own property was not given by God for humans to exploit. Ownership and cultivation had to be *just*. Consider, for example, John Winthrop's "Reasons to Be Considered for Justifying the Intended Plantation in New England and for Encouraging Such Whose Hearts God Shall Move to Join with Them in It":

> The whole earth is the Lord's garden and he hath given it to the sons of men, with a general condition, Genesis 1:28: Increase and multiply, replenish the earth and subdue it, which was again renewed to Noah. The end is double moral and natural, that man might enjoy the fruits of the earth and God might have his due glory from the creature. . . . That which lies common and hath never been replenished or subdued is free to any that will possess and improve it, for God hath given to the sons of men a double right to the earth: there is a natural and a civil right; the first right was natural when men held the earth in common, every man sowing and feeding where he pleased, and then as men and the cattle increased, they appropriated certain parcels of ground by enclosing and peculiar manurance and this in time gave them a civil right. Such was the right when Ephron the Hittite had in the field of Machpelah, wherein Abraham could not bury a dead corpse without leave, though for the out parts of the country which lay common, he dwelt upon them and took the fruit of them at his pleasure.[7]

Our natural right to benefit from the earth was considered part of the general bequest of God's bounty, and the right to own

---

7. Winthrop, "Reasons to Be Considered for Justifying the Intended Plantation in New England," 72–73.

land as property stemmed from the divine invitation to flourish. For this reason, the land was not to be manipulated for individual gain, but rather it was to be respected and farmed *for the flourishing of the community*. On these points Winthrop struck a theme that was further articulated by John Locke (1632–1704) in his *Second Treatise on Civil Government*.[8] Contemporary scholars vary in their estimates of John Locke's influence on early American thought. Some give prominence to Lockean economic individualism, while others resist situating Locke as the dominant voice in early America. Wherever one places him in American history, there is a sense in which Locke was simply one voice articulating the view that all things belong to God and that God underwrites the property claims of individuals and groups insofar as they exercise God-given powers. Like Winthrop, Locke appealed to the common good to restrict the use of civil property (there had to be enough land for the private use of others; there could not be an ownership right that would leave others impoverished) and ensure proper cultivation of land. Locke also endeavored to refine the application of appealing to divine ownership; God gave no supreme, unchecked authority to the monarchy over its subjects, to parents over children (contra Sir Robert Filmer), or to persons over their own bodies (thus, Locke objected to suicide on the grounds that it was the destruction of something owed to God). This conception of natural and civil ownership was not limited to Christian thinkers, but was also upheld by deists such as Thomas Paine (1737–1809).

> Though every man, as an inhabitant of the earth, is a joint proprietor of it in its natural state, it does not follow that he is a joint proprietor of the cultivated earth. The additional value made by cultivation, after the system was admitted, became the property of those who did it, or who inherited it from them, or who purchased it. . . . Cultivation is, at least, one of the greatest natural improvements ever made by human invention. It has given to created earth a ten-fold value.[9]

8. For a good overview of the racist elements in Locke's work, see Valls, "Locke, Slavery, and the Two Treatises."

9. Paine, "Agrarian Justice" 399–400.

So, the acquisition of goods through labor was secondary to the more fundamental entitlement that all people had to the earth by virtue of creation. The early theological treatments of divine ownership emphasized two features of the philosophy of God that deserve outlining: monotheism and divine omnipresence. The dominant view was that no other gods existed, and thus there was no alternative to God's overarching, primary claim to all of creation. The oceans, forests, and Native Americans as well as settlers were all God's. Furthermore, insofar as God was an omnipresent reality, there was no place in creation where one might possibly achieve isolation from God. The harshness of frontier and pioneer life, with their blends of hunting, farming, and self-defense, was thus understood within a broader context of a great frontier with God. There was no supremely private sector (*res privato*) in creation where one might flee from God's presence. To God, everything was public (*res publica*). While this appeal to creation established a theoretical foundation for respect and community, the second aspect of colonial, covenant theology set up the community such that its members were called to live in fellowship with Christ. According to much early American theology—Puritan, Anglican, and Roman Catholic—human beings have fallen from grace and are in need of a relation with Christ, both corporate and individual, to effect atonement with God. Calvinists in Geneva and Puritans in New England might have held a more radical view of the effects of the fall than, say, Catholics in Rome or Anglicans in Canterbury, but all understood the need for divine grace. And the Puritans made this need a crucial point as they forged their covenantal theology of regeneration and the rites and expectations of that renewal. This theology of regeneration had both an individual and a community-based component. Perhaps one of the most compelling statements of this theology of creation and regeneration is John Winthrop's famous sermon from 1630, "A Model of Christian Charity," delivered aboard the ship Arbella prior to its landing in Massachusetts Bay. This process of regeneration begins with the regeneration of the individual sinner, which then proceeds to enable the individual to love his brethren. As Winthrop describes, God works in the heart of the regenerate person to frame "these affections of love in the heart which will as natively bring forth [works of mercy]."[10] Once such regeneration of the individual has formed bonds of love between individuals, this extends to the community as a whole. Winthrop calls on all of us

> to restrain greed and to remain . . . knit more nearly to-
> gether in the bonds of brotherly affection. . . . There are
> two rules whereby we are to walk one towards another;
> justice and mercy. . . . We must delight in each other,
> make others' conditions our own, rejoice together, mourn
> together, labor and suffer together, always having before
> our eyes our commission and community in the work,
> our community as members of the same body. So shall we
> keep the unity of the spirit in the bond of peace.[11]

Nine years before Winthrop, Robert Cushman argued that God called for a communitarian ethic in an oration he delivered to the Plymouth colonists on December 9, 1621, "Sermon Describing the Sin and Danger of Self-Love." Comparing self-interested, natural-policy behavior to the "fashion of hogs," Cushman asserted that,

> A good man will not eat his morsels alone, especially, if
> he have better than others, but if by God's providence,
> he have gotten some meat which is better than ordinary,
> and better than his other brethren, he can have no rest in
> himself, except he make others partake with him. But a
> belly-god will slop all in his own throat, yea, though his
> neighbor come in and behold him eat, yet his griple-gut
> shameth not to swallow all.[12]

In light of this covenantal promise, individual human lives were to be both animated and partly defined by the welfare of others. This interwoven identity had affective and practical dimensions. According to Winthrop, economic welfare was to be

10. Winthrop, "A Model of Christian Charity," 86.

11. Winthrop, "A Model of Christian Charity," 83, 91.

12. Cushman, "Sermon Describing the Sin and Danger of Self-Love," 199.

understood in terms of a greater divine economy on which we all depend, an economy more akin to something organic and alive than to a machine. Reflecting on the nature of human social order, Winthrop gave primacy first to individual persons and then to labor, securing a profoundly humanistic point of reference.

> First for the persons. We are a company professing ourselves fellow members of Christ, in which respect only though we were absent from each other many miles, and had other imployments as far distant, yet we ought to account ourselves knit together by this bond of love, and live in the exercise of it, if we would have comfort of our being in Christ. . . . Secondly for the work we have in hand. It is by a mutual consent, through a special overvaluing providence and a more than an ordinary approbation of the churches of Christ, to seek out a place of cohabitation and consortship under a due form of government both civil and ecclesiastical. In such cases as this, the care of the public must oversway all private respects, by which not only conscience but mere civil policy cloth bind us.[13]

Which is to say that *the ends of our work are to be put towards the service of people, not the other way around.* The privileging of public good and regeneration was further advanced in the covenantal theology of John Eliot (1604–1690), Richard Baxter (1615–1691), Cotton Mather (1663–1728), and Peter Bulkeley (1717–1800), among many others, even receiving poetic idealization in Timothy Dwight's (1752–1817) *Greenfield Hill.* One sees sermons and tracts struggling to define and restrain what were seen as unfairly covetous settlements and acts, evidence that this covenantal appeal was not merely an idle ploy. Parishes reluctantly gave way to the expansion of settlements by "outlivers" and "outdwellers" (frequently farmers), but often only while admonishing individuals to avoid vice and to recall the greater community of regeneration. The colossal effort in these sermons and tracts to guide and educate would have been unintelligible if not for the successes of covenantal life.

13. Winthrop, "A Model of Christian Charity", 89.

It is within this deeply theological basis that the commons was conceived. *The commons*, in which the meadows, and much property, was shared in common, *is the expression of this ideal in which the interests of the individual are inseparably linked with and subordinated to the interests of the whole.* With these all-encompassing spiritual ties, the colonists' bonds with the others in the community, and with the community as a whole, could not be restricted to their private lives, but took form in the economic, social, and political spheres of their lives as well. Only then could the regeneration of the individual and the community truly occur. While the emphasis this theology of regeneration placed on the positive duty of the colonists to promote the common good established the foundation for their society to be driven by more than self-serving profit, it was a belief in the limits of regeneration that provided the theological support for this stress on the common good to take the form it did.

The Jeffersonian model of virtue (discussed in the introduction, where we noted its flaws) is grounded in the Enlightenment principle of the *perfectibility of human nature.* In Jefferson's agrarian ideal, under particular circumstances—namely, as farmers—humans will be inclined toward virtue. External constraints on this freedom are likely to cause vicious, destructive, or sinful behavior. By contrast, the Puritan theology of regeneration taught that human nature was essentially *fallen* and corrupt, and that human perfection would never occur in this life. Leaders, such as Increase Mather, expressed continual concern that the colonists were persisting in sin and were in need of reformation. In 1679, Mather exhorted the colonists of New England to avert God's judgment by turning from their sins, which included "pride," "a refusing to be subject to divine appointment," "contention," and many more.[14] With this understanding of human nature, humans could not be expected to act virtuously when left alone; rather, they were in need of continual spiritual instruction and civil restraint. For this reason, in the Puritan model *external constraints on action—so long as the constraints are directed toward the good—do not so much*

14. Cotton Mather, *The Christian Philosopher*, 17.

limit virtue as curb vice, ultimately promoting virtue. Thus, governmental and community constraints on the individual's freedom was essential to limit humans' naturally self-seeking behavior.

Instead of understanding their relationship to the land as something contingent, based merely on their own choosing, many of the early colonists believed they were directed to the New World by special providence. One such example is the famous depiction of the Americas by Peter Bulkeley in "The Gospel Covenant" (1639–40):

> We are as a city set upon an hill, in the open view of all the earth; the eyes of the world are upon us because we profess ourselves to be a people in covenant with God, and therefore not only the Lord our God, with whom we have made covenant, but heaven and earth, angels and men, that are witnesses of our profession, will cry shame upon us, if we walk contrary to the covenant which we have professed and promised to walk in. If we open the mouths of men against our profession by reason of the scandal of our lives, we (of all men) shall have the greater sin.[15]

In addition to such flights of high prose, many other works chronicled God's special acts of providence in guiding the colonists to establish a society dedicated to God. One that is often referred to by scholars is Increase Mather's (1639–1723) *An Essay for the Recording of Illustrious Providences*. Robert Cushman (1579–1625) also heralded the guidance of God in "Reasons and Considerations Touching the Lawfulness of Removing Out of England into the Parts of America," as did G. Mourt with *Relation* (1622); ("Mourt" is a pseudonym and the identity of the author is not known), and William Bradford (1590–1657) in *Of Plymouth Plantation*. Meanwhile, others worried that the God-oriented life intended by God was imperiled, a concern that may be traced in Peter Bulkeley's "The Gospel Covenant" and Edward Johnson's (1598–1672) *Wonder-Working Providence of Zion's Savior in New England*. All of the above titles document the wide-ranging conviction that the colonies were to be viewed *sub specie aeternitatis*. Bulkeley used the

---

15. Bulkeley, "The Gospel Covenant," 120.

image of a city on a hill rather than a farm on the plain, but what he, Winthrop, and others pointed to was an integrated form of life that was satisfying not only to individuals, but to the greater polity and to God. Thus, the farmer, the carpenter, and the cleric had their roles in what Perry Miller has effectively described as a Great Chain of Being in the early colonies (recalling the medieval notion and the related notions of plenitude which applaud the fecundity of goods—*bonum est multiplex*).[16] On this model, human beings found themselves in a good creation, and were called to assume their role of responsibility among the vast expanse of creation.

> Out of the same being [God] have proceeded the stars, animals, men; but in some incarnations the being has taken forms superior to others. "The least spear of grass has the same power to make it that made heaven and angels," says the Puritan, but he does not then chant with the author of *Leaves of Grass* that the least thing in creation is equal to any other. A fly is above the cedar because it has another life which the cedar has not, "so the meanest believer is better than the most glorious hypocrite." In the regenerate, the author of all life ordains yet another life superior to the other forms, giving them something that the others have not. In the course of providence God often provides men with powers and gifts, bridles their violence, overcomes their pride, teaches them the truth of Scripture, but these things He does by managing secondary causes, sending men to the right teachers, instructing them through their experience or through science.[17]

Science, moral education, and humane teaching all had roles in further mobilizing and directing the human function within God's creation. One may object that this view of creation clashes with seventeenth- and eighteenth-century New England teachings about human depravity. Indeed, it is difficult to find Puritan joy in the goods of creation upon reading Jonathan Edwards's (1703–1758) extraordinary "Sinners in the Hands of an Angry God"

16. See Miller, *The New England Mind*.
17. Miller, *The New England Mind*, 211.

sermon or Thomas Hooker's *The Soul's Preparation for Christ*. But the predominant depiction of human sin displayed in the Great Awakening—perhaps the high-water mark for American teaching on depravity—was often contrasted with the beauty of both God and creation. One would be hard-pressed to find a greater exaltation of divine beauty than is articulated in Edwards's mature theological writing. Edwards et al. deemed sin a grave splinter at the heart of creation because it was a violation of the fecundity of a world meant to be rightly enjoyed in accordance with divine ordinances. Despite a robust theology of depravity and the hardships of early colonial life, little searching is required to find praise of God for the abundance of trees, wild food, and good soil. Hunting showed God's grandeur, for colonial hunters were able to directly access from creation bounties of turkey, goose, duck, partridge, caribou, moose, bear, deer, lobster, fish, clams, and oysters. This bounty may have furthered a feeling of shame at failing to deserve God's gifts, but it also highlighted God's generosity. God diffused goodness all through the creation (*Bonum deffusivum sui*). Arguably, the final Puritan disposition was a kind of cosmic optimism that regarded nature as fundamentally good and clung to the hope that sinners might repent, undergo regeneration, and live justly. The sheer breadth of the ensuing European immigration posed a challenge to this effort to see America as the new Zion. This sketch of early colonial thought emphasizes Puritan settlements, but waves of migration quickly established significant religious diversity. In addition to migrations of Roman Catholics, the colonies had an influx from a wide array of Protestant faiths: Anglican, Baptist, Congregational, Lutheran, Presbyterian, Quaker (or the Religious Society of Friends). The glorious image of America as a great just city on a hill was undermined by episodes of religious persecution. The religious fervor of some of the early American preaching also sparked conflicts, such as the strife between New Light and Old Light movements, the controversy over the Halfway Covenant, and the impassioned debates concerning predestination between adherents Calvinism and Arminianism. Most disturbing of all was the failure of the early Christian colonists of all denominations (except some of the Quakers) in the seventeenth and eighteenth centuries to consistently respect Native American entitlements to both land and labor, and—a tragedy whose effects we are still experiencing—the intolerance and dehumanization of Africans through the practice of slavery. In 1790, the southern United States had a total population of 1,961,000, including 657,327 slaves. In the midst of these grave injustices, it is difficult to ferret out a constructive, positive vision of the goodness of creation and justice. Still, one can see in the extant colonial books, tracts, sermons, diaries, and covenants some of the great themes and principles of justice and fairness outlined above. And these themes and principles would be refined and used to condemn the legacy of exploitation in the colonies and the early American Republic.

## Minds and Bodies in the New England Colonies

Our last section highlights the broad theme of a God-given integration of labor and land, governed by notions of the common good. It may seem that Christian theology in the colonies would have prevented the wayward mind-body dualism that some contemporary agrarians complain about. In *The Agrarian Vision*, for example, Paul Thompson laments the dualist view of mind and body as distinct entities, arguing that it is in profound conflict with the more embedded way in which humans exist in the world.[18] We propose that in a theistic framework, there was a profound integration of person or mind and body that underscored a robust agrarianism. In the next section we note that theism did indeed serve to ameliorate such dualities, and in a final section, "Farming and the Mind of God," we lay out an understanding of farming that integrates colonial land and labor practices in a theistic framework. But just as the profession of Christian theism did not prevent certain ills—some of them mild but others so grave that their scars are still with us—it did not altogether smooth over the philosophical tension between the duality of mind and body. In what follows we

18. Thompson, *The Agrarian Vision*, chapter 6.

note in very broad terms how the colonists sometimes gave primacy to physical bodies and an inchoate materialism and sometimes took to the opposite task, by giving such prominence to the mind that full-blown philosophical idealism—broadly, the view that the world is fundamentally mental, or immaterial—flourished in the major colonial colleges.

The colonists' preoccupation with meeting the material needs of their settlements went hand in glove with the emphasis placed by colonial colleges on science, both theoretical and applied. Isaac Newton's (1642–1727) works were widely used in the colleges, and the American contributions to Newton's work, while meager (for example, Newton duly recorded Harvard's Thomas Brattle sighting the comet of 1680), were viewed as a small sign of American promise. Newton's laws were regarded as the clearest, most systematic guide to the structure of the cosmos, and were held in such esteem that Newton, along with John Locke, was generally singled out as one of the leading lights in early American scientific thought. John Locke's work on the nature of perception and matter contributed to the Newtonian goal of establishing the parameters of the physical science. Locke adopted and refined Galileo's distinction between primary and secondary qualities, delimiting the physical world in terms of size, shape, and weight, while the secondary world of color, smell, sound, and so on was identified as a human contribution to the material world as it appears to us. This philosophy of perception presented a view of nature that privileged geometry, mathematics, and quantification. Some of the first American philosophers were attracted to a materialist worldview, according to which the world is purely matter and there is no transcendent mind or soul. In *The Principles of Action in Matter*, Cadwallader Colden (1688–1776) developed a more positive conception of matter than either Locke or Newton allowed. Working from within a Newtonian framework, and in sympathy with Thomas Hobbes (1588–1679), Colden developed a conception of matter sufficiently powerful to, in theory, account for much more than either Newton or Locke had supposed. Colden construed matter in positive, potent terms; matter was not identified principally in terms of geometry and resistance, but as a causally active source that provided a rich framework for describing and explaining the world. While we shall note in the next section that Colden stopped short of a comprehensive materialism, he went quite far in that direction. Colden conceded the contingency of the present cosmos, but he was less certain about whether there was ever a time when no physical world existed. Thus, he states, "There may have been a time when the present solar system did not exist," and also, "No time can be supposed, when no system of matter did exist."[19] Other materialist elements entered the American scene by way of Joseph Priestly's work (1733–1804). Much admired by Thomas Jefferson (1743–1826), Priestly won his scientific and intellectual reputation by discovering oxygen. He later sought refuge in America to avoid prosecution for his heterodox views. Priestly argued that the mind and body are identical, also denying the existence of an afterlife, then passing the torch to his son-in-law, Thomas Cooper, who advocated materialism in his *View of the Metaphysical and Physiological Arguments in Favor of Materialism*. Like Priestly, Cooper denied the credibility of believing that there is an afterlife on the grounds that the mind and body are identical. If the mind and body are identical or inseparable, then the destruction of one (the body) seems to lead to the destruction of the other (the soul or person). While this brand of materialism may not necessitate the denial of an afterlife (some orthodox Christians at that time, as well as some today, believe the afterlife was grounded in a bodily resurrection, while others conceived of an afterlife in terms of a re-creation of embodied persons), it was judged by many contemporaries to challenge belief in an afterlife and thus to threaten the moral and religious groundwork of civil society. Benjamin Rush (1746–1813) advocated a material understanding of human character and moral decision-making. In *Influence of Physical Causes upon the Moral Faculty*, Rush argued for the physical underpinnings of the mind and the importance of empirical inquiry into origins of human moral action. Joseph Buchanan (1785–1829) also endeavored to develop a scientific, material account of human thought and

19. Colden, *The Principles of Action in Matter*, 165.

action in his *Philosophy of Human Nature*. Like Priestly, Cooper, and others drawn to a materialist view of human nature, he denied individual immortality. French materialism had an impact on colonial thinkers through the works of Etienne Bonnot de Condillac (1715–1780), Claude-Adrien Helvetius (1715–1771), and Baron d'Holbach (1723–1789). While matter and materialism had an influence on colonial thought, the greater emphasis was on the mind and the development of either a dualist or idealist philosophy. In *Philosophical Ideas in the United States*, Harvey Townsend gives idealism the edge. There is one dominant note in American philosophy, he says, namely idealism.

> The word must not be taken, however, either as an epithet of praise or as a narrowly technical label. It is intended only to characterize the central tendency in our philosophy to approximate the ancient doctrine that the visible is no whit more real than the invisible, in fact that the invisible kingdoms furnish the foundation.[20]

Harvey Townsend stressed the colonial inclination towards immaterial realities and principles in both practice and theory: "Platonism was the common possession of colonial settlers."[21] However, the general climate of the culture allowed some of the best of the colonial philosophers to articulate forms of philosophical idealism. Samuel Johnson (1696–1772), the first president of King's College in New York City (now Columbia University), was a premier colonial philosopher in his day. He, along with Jonathan Edwards, was also an idealist. Johnson was heavily influenced by the Anglo-Irish Bishop George Berkeley (1685–1753), whom he met during Berkeley's sojourn in Rhode Island. Johnson's two most noteworthy philosophical works are *An Introduction to the Study of Philosophy* and *Elementa Philosophica*. Johnson's idealism was very Berkeleyan. In his letter to Berkeley, dated February 5, 1730, Johnson writes:

---

20. Townsend, *Philosophical Ideas in the United States*, 4.
21. Townsend, *Philosophical Ideas in the United States*, 20.

> As to space and duration, I do not pretend to have any
> other notion of their exterior existence than what is nec-
> essarily implied in the notion we have of God; I do not
> suppose that they are any thing distinct from, or exterior
> to, the infinite and external mind; for I conclude with
> you that there is nothing exterior to my mind but God
> and other spirits with attributes or properties belonging
> to them and ideas contained in them.[22]

Johnson, like Berkeley, appealed to God's omnipresence and
omni-perceptiveness in explaining the existence and stability of
the world.

> But it may be asked, How do those things exist, which
> have an actual existence, but of which no created mind
> is conscious?—For instance, the Furniture of this room,
> when we are absent, and the room is shut up, and no
> created mind perceives it; How do these things exist?—I
> answer . . . in short, That the existence of these things is
> in God's supposing of them, in order to the rendering
> complete the series of things . . . which he has appointed.
> The supposition of God, which we speak of, is nothing
> else but God's acting, in the course and series of his excit-
> ing ideas, as if they (the things supposed) were in actual
> idea. . . . That which truly is the Substance of all Bodies, is
> the infinitely exact, and precise, and perfectly stable Idea
> in God's mind, together with his stable Will that the same
> shall gradually be communicated to us, and to other
> minds, according to certain fixed and exact established
> Methods and Laws.[23]

The mind of God plays a profoundly central role in the construction of the cosmos, and Johnson thus characterized nature as
the art of God. By his lights, nature is divine *techne*, and human
actions and art reflect and participate in God's power. Johnson's
philosophical idealism offered a formal framework for what Herbert Schneider has characterized as a fundamental Puritan thesis:

22. Samuel Johnson, "Letter to George Berkeley," 59.

23. Samuel Johnson, "Letter to George Berkeley," 75–76.

> Eupraxia, or skill, exhibited in the works (*euprassomena*)
> of God or man was the basic category of philosophic
> analysis and enabled the Puritans to interpret their arts
> and crafts, including the most mercantile and menial, in
> the perspective of God's will.[24]

Therefore, Johnson's philosophy may be viewed as a formalized extension of the Puritan emphasis on the primacy of will and activity in the very constitution of the world. Solidifying the place of philosophical idealism in the American philosophical tradition is the man most often hailed as America's first philosopher of European rank: Jonathan Edwards. Edwards also propounded a strongly Platonic philosophy of God. For Edwards, God's excellence and perfection was a supreme, unsurpassable beauty, with the external, material world itself a reflection of the mind of God.

> As to Bodies . . . they are the communications of the
> Great Original Spirit; and doubtless, in metaphysical
> strictness and propriety, He is, as there is none else. He
> is likewise Infinitely Excellent, and all Excellence and
> Beauty is derived from him, in the same manner as all
> Being. And in all other Excellence is, in strictness, only
> a shadow of His.[25]

Edwards's philosophy traces a portrait of God's regenerative covenant with humanity. This is especially apparent in his reflection on the Christian belief in the Trinity, where a kind of divine community is nested at the very heart of all existence. The Father-Son-Holy Spirit relationship calls humanity to a wider fellowship in this world and the next. From the standpoint of mind-body dualists, early colonial philosophers appeared prepared either to replace mind with body or vice versa.

---

24. Schneider, *A History of American Philosophy*, 9.
25. Edwards, "Memoirs of Jonathan Edwards," 74 75.

## The Theistic Chord

We believe Christian theism was a major factor in the stable, integrated portrait of mind and body in early colonial thought. Theism acts as a belief that serves as a check or boundary on the direction of one's reflection, a belief Nicholas Wolterstorff has called a "control belief."[26] To those favoring idealism, Christian theism underscored the goodness of the material world, and to those drawn to materialism it suggested that there was more to the cosmos than could be captured in a strictly materialist natural philosophy. On the materialist front, few colonists were prepared to argue that the full complexity, apparent design, and the bare existence of the material world was a self-explaining phenomenon. Even materialists like Thomas Hobbes conceived of a God, albeit construed along material lines. Cadwallader Colden also avoided a strict materialism:

> God in the beginning created a certain being, to which he gave the power of motion; and distributed this being, in certain proportions, in the several parts of the universe. The granting of this is no negative to the existence of spirits; they may, and undoubtedly both exist, without including any contradiction.[27]

Benjamin Franklin (1706–1790), Ethan Allen (1737–1789), Thomas Paine (1737–1809), and Thomas Jefferson (1743–1826) all welcomed this philosophical emphasis on the material world, though *none* of them believed in the complete sufficiency of a material explanation of the cosmos. Once one admits God, whether on deistic or theistic grounds, one opens the door to the belief that human nature itself may have non-materialist features. To many, d'Holbach's picture of human beings as machines and Hobbes's dismissal of consciousness appeared to ignore the reality of thoughts and feelings commonly considered part of what makes human beings created in God's image. In noting how Christian theism restrained full-scale materialism, it should be added that

26. Wolterstorff, *Reason Within the Bounds of Religion*, 63.
27. Mayer, *A History of American Thought*, 69.

Christian theism was not generally considered an obstacle to science in the colonies. In the early colleges, scientific inquiry was often construed as a natural, good exercise of religious investigation. It was thought that by studying nature, one thereby studied the mind of God. So, in his great work *The Christian Philosopher*, Cotton Mather extols the uniformity and design of the universe as a thing to be investigated to the glory of God. "The works of the Glorious GOD in the Creation of the World, are what I now propose to exhibit."[28] The text reads like a mix of early science and ecstatic celebration of nearly all of the natural world: "Even the most noxious and most abject of the Vegetables, how useful they are!" Though idealism achieved celebrity with Johnson, Edwards, and Berkeley, its reign was short. At Princeton, for example, idealism was taught as an authoritative theory only briefly before it was supplanted by the commonsense philosophy of those trained in the Scottish Enlightenment. In a sense, the Scottish philosophers Thomas Reid (1710–1796), Dugald Stewart (1753–1828), and others appreciated the idealist emphasis on mind, yet also the materialist's physical world. Reid's mind-body dualism is perhaps the most compelling of the period. According to Reid, the mind-independent nature of the material world is evident to humans in perception. Moreover, he argued that explanation of the material world as entirely constituted by the mental failed to recognize the goodness of the material world as created by God. Earlier, we noted the agrarian Paul Thompson's unhappiness with dualism. Thompson ties (we believe wrongly) dualism to the image of positing a ghost (i.e., the mind) in the machine (i.e., the body). This caricature—made famous by Gilbert Ryle (1900–1976)—is indeed a caricature and does an injustice to the way many dualists advance an integrated understanding of embodiment. In the theistic climate of the colonies, some of the worries that would later be articulated by Ryle and Thompson were addressed. We will briefly consider colonial reasoning on mind-body dualism and the challenges of metaphysics, ethics, and epistemology.

28. Cotton Mather, *The Christian Philosopher*, 11.

Regarding the mind-body interaction, many colonial thinkers appealed to the greater power of God in explaining how any causal relations could exist whatsoever. If one begins with an entirely materialist concept of the cosmos it is difficult to explain the emergence of any immaterial reality. But if one remains open to the possibility that the very nature of the material world stems from God, the existence of mind and the nature of mind-body interaction can be placed into an integrative scheme. While an idealist, Johnson articulated such mind-body interaction along dualist line in *Elementa Philosophica*:

> We are, at present, spirits or minds connected with gross, tangible bodies in such a manner, that as our bodies, can perceive and act nothing but by our minds, so, on the other hand, our minds perceive and act by means of our bodily organs. Such is the present law of our nature, which I conceive to be no other than a mere arbitrary constitution or establishment of Him that hath made us to be what we are. And accordingly I apprehend that the union between our souls and bodies, during our present state, consists in nothing else but this law of our nature, which is the will and perpetual fiat of that infinite Parent Mind, who made us, and holds our souls in life, and in whom we live, and move, and have our being, viz., that our bodies should be thus acted by our minds, and that our minds should thus perceive and act by the organs of our bodies, and under such limitations as in fact we find ourselves to be attended with.[29]

To some materialist critics, the appeal to God in explaining mind-body interaction may appear an explanation of the obscure in terms of the more obscure (*obscurum per obscurius*). But contemporary physicists over two hundred years after Johnson's death have yet to reach a consensus on a theory of the ultimate constituents of the physical world, while a theistic account of both the physical and mental world would place mind-body interaction within a comprehensive, unified framework.

29. Samuel Johnson, "Letter to George Berkeley," 66.

Consider the ethical problem of dualism. Does mind-body dualism denigrate the body? While some dualists have treated the body as a prison or bare habitation (e.g., Pythagoras), surely this isn't necessary. If the mind and body are both deemed creations of a good God, and if God's incarnation unites God with a physical body, then it seems odd to view the body as something base and worthless.

Consider finally the epistemological concern: if mind and body are separate, how shall we guarantee our knowledge of other minds? On this front, colonial Puritans dramatically proposed that we may not have such a guarantee but by the grace of God. Puritans had reservations and were generally skeptical about both our access to the interior lives of others and our own self-knowledge based in introspection. A result of sin and the fall, we may even be able to mask our true intentions from ourselves. In this regard, mind-body dualism actually fits the moral data better than philosophies of mind that deny the existence of an interior subjective world. In the absence of sin and in a state of grace, we might well have lucid, unimpeded access to our own minds and, due to the wholly good disclosure of others, access to theirs as well. But sin still haunts these claims. Alan Heimert and Andrew Delbanco summarize the Puritan position: "If the Catholic question had been 'what shall I do to be saved?' and the question of the Reformers became 'how shall I know if I am saved?' perhaps the American Puritans asked, more eventually, 'What am I in the eyes of God?'"[30]

We believe this God-eye orientation is the key; it is from the God's eye point of view of colonial thought that we find a harmony between the mind and the body and some of the other dualities Ryle and Thompson would protest in the twentieth century. In an overriding theistic context, one finds an integral understanding of the mind and body. If the mind and body were in a sense integrated, however uneasily, in pre-Revolutionary America, what of agriculture and the larger understanding of the role of society, the relationship between the individual and nature, a person's land and labor?

30. Heimert and Delbanco (eds.), *The Puritans in America*, 15.

## Mapping the Material World

While mind and body found some kind of integration in the theology and philosophy undergirding New England colonial society, the material world of New England was itself understood according to the principles of the physiocratic school of economic thought. The physiocrats, credited as having developed the first comprehensive economic system of thought, held that the wealth of nations did not depend on international trade surpluses, as argued by the mercantilists. Rather, they saw agriculture as the source of national wealth. As argued by François Quesnay (1694–1774), the recognized founder of this school of thought,

> Let the sovereign and the nation never lose sight of the fact that the earth is the sole source of all riches, and that it is agriculture which multiplies riches. For it is the augmentation of riches that assures the wealth of the population; men and wealth cause agriculture to prosper, extend commerce, animate industry, increase and perpetuate all wealth. Upon that abundant source of wealth, agriculture, depends the success of all the parties concerned in the administration of the kingdom.[31]

According to the physiocrats, only land was able to generate rent, that is, a surplus above payments to labor and capital. Manufacturers could promote their own interest and profits, but their efforts did not add in any substantial way to the riches of the state. As manufacturers only modify something that it already in existence, nothing new is created by the act of manufacturing. The sale of a manufactured good merely transfers funds from the buyer to the seller; no new revenue, no new wealth is created. Therefore, argue the physiocrats, the land, and only the land, is "incontrovertibly the sole source of all riches."[32]

Such an economic philosophy resonated with the land-loving, farm-dwelling New England settlers, although Ben Franklin

---

31. Quesnay, "General Maxims of the Economical Government in an Agricultural Kingdom," 394.

32. Malthus, "An Essay on the Principle of Population," 19.

stands out among the American physiocrats as the most zealous. Having been introduced to the school of thought during his first visit to Paris in 1767, Franklin became thoroughly convinced of its merit as a means of understanding the economy, writing to a friend in 1768 that,

> The true source of riches is husbandry. Agriculture is truly productive of new wealth; manufacturers only change forms, and whatever value they give to the materials they work upon, they in the meantime consume an equal value in provisions, &c. so that riches are not increased by manufacturing.[33]

A year later, Franklin made an even stronger case for an agriculturally based economy, by linking agriculture not only to wealth, but also to virtue. In *Positions to be Examined, Concerning National Wealth* (1769), Franklin wrote,

> There seem to be but three ways for a nation to acquire wealth. The first is by *war* as the Romans did in plundering their conquered neighbors. This is *robbery*. The second by *commerce* which is generally *cheating*. The third by *agriculture,* the only *honest way*; wherein man receives a real increase of the seed thrown into the ground, in a kind of continual miracle wrought by the hand of God in his favour, as a reward for his innocent life, and virtuous industry.[34]

As an economic model, physiocratic thought took direct aim at the mercantilism that represented the prevailing perspective on the source of national wealth. In place of the physiocratic view that wealth literally springs from the ground, the mercantilist thought that a nation's wealth depended directly on its trade. Unlike the southern colonies with their export-based economies, mercantilist thought never really caught on in New England. As a way of

33. Franklin, Benjamin. *The Papers of Benjamin Franklin,* vol. 15, January 1 through December 31, 1768, ed. William B. Willcox. New Haven and London: Yale University Press, 1972, 51–53.

34. Franklin, "Positions to be Examined, Concerning National Wealth" 144.

understanding one's place in the material world, the physiocratic model more closely reflected the lived economy of rural settlements, dependent as they were on whatever riches they could harvest from the ground.

## Farming and the Mind of God

Let us return to Hurt's argument. Is Hurt right? We believe there is mixed evidence. Economic gain was certainly pivotal in early American life, and this was as true in agriculture as in anything else. Alan Heimert and Andrew Delbanco put it dramatically: "To say that the early settlements of New England included or tolerated merchant activity is badly to underestimate the case. It is more accurate to say that the first English settlements were merchant activities."[35] True, it is difficult to imagine that the Virginia Company of London was moved by anything but self-interest. But can merchant activities, commercial agriculture, or family farms exist without a culture, without an overarching framework of how to understand one's self and the land? There are conceptual reasons for finding this absurd.

The very practice of agriculture entails certain philosophical commitments, regarding (to give just a short list) the notion of property, the reasons we can be confident that crops will grow each year, the value of the crops produced, and the ultimate reasons why we *should* farm. Insofar as we try to reconstruct sympathetically what it was like to farm in a colonial cultural context, we are led to conclude that farming was done *sub specie aeternitatis*, and assessed *ordine ad universum*. However imperfectly executed, there were strong religious threads bolstering a model of stewardship that situated and secured farming as an act ordained by God in a good creation. Early farming was not so much conceived of as an activity within a "moral economy" as opposed to something within a system of "commercial agriculture." Rather, we imagine it was largely intended to fit both.

35. Heimart and Delbanco (eds.), *The Puritans in America*, 185.

The vast examples of pious literature cited above, the existence of counsels of stewardship in sermons and essays, prevalent biblical teaching, etc., all contribute to the construction of a picture of farmers who understood their vocation (including economic exchange) in the context of a generally theistic cosmos. The appeal to theism at many points may be no more than lip service, but it is challenging to explain it away entirely as a bare accessory to the mercantile lives of the colonists. From the colonial theological standpoint, Christian theism provided a guarantor for farming. The art of farming was a reflection of the art of God. In biblical texts, God is a farmer, planting a garden in Eden (Gen 2); God blesses harvests and is called upon in prayer for rain (e.g., Elijah's prayer for rain in 1 Kgs 18:41–46); God is a sower, planting the word of God (Matt 13:1–23); Jesus is even first mistaken for a gardener after the resurrection (John 20:15); the church is fed with bread and wine, fruits of the earth harvested through labor. All of this teaching, broadcast from colonial pulpits, served as the guarantor of the reason and industry that the farmer expended. In some regard, theism underwrote the entire enterprise.

Reason was an important tool to the farmer. What is the source of reason itself? How do we have confidence in it? As the Cambridge Platonists argued, reason is trustworthy insofar as it is "the Light of Lord." The reason why the Cambridge Platonists, especially Henry More (1614–1687) and Ralph Cudworth (1617–1688), achieved such popularity in the colonies is because they (like the Scottish school of common sense) attributed the reliability of reason to the mind and purposes of a good God. Farmers, as well as merchants, mathematicians, and politicians, could trust reason because it originated with God. The mind of a farmer made in God's image was trustworthy because of the supremely good, anterior mind of God.

Just as an explanation of the rise of modern science requires a serious treatment of the event's philosophical context (whether it be in scholastic theism or in the Renaissance revival of Greek humanism), one also needs to take the context of these exchanges and agricultural practices seriously. Miller does well to point out how sciences in the colonies were bolstered by faith. Science was not merely *tolerated* because faith was believed to be secure whatever physics or astronomy might teach, but it was actually *advanced* as a part of faith itself, a positive declaration of the will of God, a necessary and indispensable complement to biblical revelation. The same is true for agriculture. *Christian theism helped provide an integral framework, however imperfect, for the conception of land and labor, mind and body, self and nature.* It may well be true that Timothy Dwight's poetry was idealized, and that Jared Eliot's (1685–1763) *Essays on Field Husbandry* might have fallen on deaf ears, and that Dickinson's 1764 "Farmer's Letter" may have dealt more with political theory than agriculture, and that Thomas Paine's *Agrarian Justice* could have been advanced just as well without a single reference to God. But we argue that all the emphasis placed by the colonists on the mind of God and its integral role in holding the cosmos together was not empty rhetoric, but rather helped set a standard for a responsible, wise colonial agriculture carried out for the common good.

To conclude, we make the point that reclaiming an agrarian vision today means inviting theology or philosophy back into the agricultural context. While the case study of the New England colonies demonstrates the practical possibility of conceiving of agricultural activities in philosophical terms, we argue that on some level, it is impossible *not* to frame our understanding of the land in terms of an underlying philosophy. Instead of explaining our relationship with the land in purely economic terms, it is not conceptually possible to avoid committing ourselves to certain philosophical positions. As we must hold to some philosophy within which to understand the individual and communal practice of agriculture, adopting an agrarian philosophy inspired by that of the New England colonies is an option that is both viable and desirable. In a sense, the agrarian vision manifested in the commons was a product of the particular theological context of seventeenth-century New England. The explicit formulation of the relationship between God, the colonists, and the land was deeply grounded in Puritan covenantal theology.

However, this agrarian vision was neither entirely isolated from nor completely incompatible with other philosophical ideas discussed in America and England at the time. Contrary to the contentions of those such as Paul Thompson, each major metaphysical theory regarding the existence of and the relation between mind and matter in colonial New England—the dominant philosophy of dualism alongside nascent philosophies of materialism and idealism—had room for an agrarian conception of a communitarian property ethic as well as a deep valuing of the land. As such, we believe that agrarianism can accommodate the array of diverse philosophies prevalent in the pluralistic landscape of contemporary America. In a society that lacks the broad theological and philosophical unity of the New England colonies, surely any agrarian program must be compatible with a variety of metaphysical positions. This need not, and indeed cannot, crumble every particular philosophical or theological foundation for agrarianism; these must be preserved. Instead, we need to look for common ground in a variety of philosophical traditions. While formulating and practicing a widely appealing account of agrarianism that still preserves particular metaphysical groundings is certainly a challenge, it is one we must face in order to address the host of issues confronting the agricultural industry today. Using the commons as a model for contemporary agrarianism, we believe that adopting such an agrarian vision is possible, and moreover, it is *necessary* to face contemporary challenges.

Chapter Two

---

# An Economic Characterization of the Commons in New England Agrarianism

We are knit together as a body in a most strict and sacred
bond and covenant of the Lord, of the violation whereof
we make great conscience, and by virtue whereof we hold
ourselves straitly tied to all care of each other's good.

—William Bradford, citing letter from
John Robinson and Willam Bruster.[1]

Heaven is under our feet as well as over our heads.

—Henry David Thoreau[2]

IN CONTRAST TO THE current emphasis given by many contemporary agrarian writers to individual freedom, the New
England agrarian tradition as practiced from the founding of
the Plymouth Colony in the early seventeenth century through

1. Bradford, *Bradford's History of the Plymouth Settlement, 1608–1650*, 28.
2. Thoreau, *Walden*, 274.

the mid-eighteenth century consistently emphasizes the need for individual self-seeking behavior to be constrained in pursuit of the common good. One hundred and sixty years before Jefferson celebrated the virtues of the independent yeoman farmer, Robert Cushman warned the planters at Plymouth to avoid the temptations offered by a "belly-god" to "preferre their owne matters," and instead strive "to be joynted together and knit by flesh and synewes, . . . [bearing] one anothers burthen," with justice in distribution ultimately adjudicated by "law and governors."[3]

As New England's agrarianism is reflected in the town charters of colonial New England's towns and villages, it honors the term's original roots as concerns the just distribution of land. Justice in distribution and assured access to the means of production is at the heart of the original understanding of agrarianism. Justice in distribution was achieved by creating a set of laws and practices assuring that all members of a community could share in the resource base necessary for their survival. Borrowing from Locke, the New England commons existed as an institution focused on assuring that an individual's use or appropriation of God's gifts of land and its produce was constrained so that "enough, and as good" was available for all members of the community.[4] Writing about the open-field system incorporated into the initial design of Sudbury, Massachusetts, Sumner Powell notes that "No one was to exclude a neighbor from such a necessity as good meadow, or the down, or the woods. And if anyone practiced such exclusion, or attempted to increase the amount of his holding at the expense of his neighbors, all villagers reacted instantly to restore their 'rights.'"[5] The New England commons was not a manifestation of communism, or even socialism.[6] It was not instituted to assure equal shares to individuals of unequal talent and varying levels of industriousness.

3. Cushman, "A Sermon Preached at Plimmoth in New-England December 9, 1621," 9, 25, and 26.
4. Locke, "The Second Treatise: An Essay Concerning the True Original, Extent, and End of Civil Government" in *Two Treatises of Government*, 112.
5. Powell, *Puritan Village*, 10.
6. See Zernike, "The Pilgrims Were . . . , Socialists?"

Rather, it was instituted to assure all members access to the productive resources of the land to the extent that they could have as much as they would need to survive and participate in society. Neither individual survival nor prosperity were guaranteed under this system, but at least the *means to survival* were guaranteed.[7]

The commons follows directly from a theological understanding of Christ's calling to his followers to live as a community of diversely talented and industrious individuals who are nonetheless knit together by the bonds of Christian love. Furthermore, and perhaps most importantly, given the Puritan's recognition of what Puritans would call sin, and what we might recognize today as narrowly defined self-interest, the Puritans were not content to rely on mere exhortation to elicit the community-wide efforts necessary to assure the availability of a complete means of subsistence to all community members. Rather, the commons existed as a physical, political, and economic entity whose continued existence required intensive investment of communal labor, political compromise, bureaucratic skill, and legislative action. In stark contrast to the libertarian ideals of the Jeffersonian agrarians and their descendants, New England's agrarianism—its commitment to justice in the distribution of the fruits of the God-given earth—required careful coordination, even-handed oversight, community-wide support, and near-constant enforcement.

References to New England's system of common fields, meadows, pastures, and woodlots found in its town charters from the seventeenth to the eighteenth centuries reflect an understanding that those resources necessary for survival needed to be shared, and their use regulated. This idea persisted for centuries. Even as late as 1859, Henry David Thoreau argued that "We hear of cow-commons and ministerial lots, but we want men-commons and lay lots, inalienable forever. Let us keep the New World new, preserve all the advantages of living in the country. There is meadow and

---

7. While the London-based investors in Plymouth Colony may well have insisted on commonly held assets as a means of reducing their risk in this far-flung enterprise, the Massachusetts-based settlers needed to band together to reduce the more immediate risk of extermination.

pasture and wood-lot for the town's poor. Why not a forest and huckleberry-field for the town's rich?"[8]

The commons, as realized among New England's settlers, existed as a practical way of assuring access to the basic requirements for survival. While the Plymouth colony privatized some of its land as well as most of its houses and livestock in 1627, the majority of the colony's acres remained as commons, as did *all* the meadowland. About the meadows, Governor Bradford writes, "But no meadows were to be laid out at all; nor were they for many years after, because of the *scarceness* of meadow land. If they had been given out now, it would have hindered later developments; so each season everyone was shown where to mow, according the proportion of cattle he had, and the fodder he required."[9]

The common field system was developed, according to Brian Donahue, to "afford broad access to the complete means of subsistence, in a world in which individual holdings were small and resources scarce. It operated not so much to extract the highest productivity from the land through specialization as to maximize security though diversification."[10] In refraining from distributing the majority of a town's meadows, fields, and woodlots as private property, New England's colonial development reflects a sensibility that held that the very scarceness of a resource critical for human survival required, as matter of justice, that these critical resources be held and managed in common.

Survival depended on forming a community that included a mix of several traits: physical endurance, certainly, but also wisdom and leadership. Procreative ability had to be tossed in too, if this wasn't going to simply be a colonial outpost set up to collect and export beaver. This necessarily diverse mix of human traits meant that there would be stronger and weaker individuals, younger and older ones, people who knew how to mend and sew, and people who knew how to fish, plant, and build. If they were *all* going to survive, critical resources needed to be available to all.

8. Thoreau, *Journal XII, March 2, 1859–November 30, 1859*, 387.

9. Bradford, *Plymouth Plantation*, 178.

10. Donahue, *The Great Meadow*, 64.

Participation in colonial New England's commons corresponds to John Rawls' description of *primary goods*, insofar as full access to the commons provided rights, liberties, opportunities, income, and wealth.[11] In colonial New England, the timberland, the meadows, the grazing land, and the surface waters were indeed recognized as primary goods, essential for survival. As such, the just community could not allow for a distribution that would exclude any of its members from access to these critical goods: to do so would be the equivalent of sentencing them to death. These essential goods, then, were part of the commons.

In Concord, where the grazing land was held in common, grazing rights were allocated to an individual based on the formula of one head of cattle (or two yearlings, or four sheep, or one horse) per twenty acres of privately owned land controlled by the individual.[12] Recognizing, however, that household subsistence required the equivalent of four cows, Concord in 1655 passed a law allowing "poor men"—which is to say, men with fewer than eighty acres of private land—to pasture at least four cows (or their equivalent in animal units) on the common grazing land.[13] Sudbury regulated not only the use of the commons for grazing, but regulated the extraction and use of all timber within the town's borders, fining individuals who failed to get permission before felling a tree.[14] Meanwhile, Braintree's town records attest to the use of the commons as defense against an ever-present existential threat. At its September, 1646 meeting, the Braintree town council passed a motion allowing for "[a] grant of taking timber off of the common for a mans (sic) own use, But not to sell out of Towne: . . . It is ordered that [e]very man that is an inhabitant of the Towne shall have Liberty to take any timber off the Common for any use in the Towne [provided] so they make not sale of it out."[15] The commons existed for survival, and not for sale.

11. Rawls, *A Theory of Justice*, 54.
12. Donahue, *The Great Meadow*, 123.
13. Donahue, *The Great Meadow*, 123.
14. Powell, *Puritan Village*, 96.
15. *Records of the Town of Braintree, 1640 to 1793*, 4.

As a means of administering justice, encroachments to the commons were vigorously prosecuted. In Sudbury, while meadow holders had the right to enclose their own meadows, should a farmer's enclosure prevent access of others' herds to the commons, the careless farmer needed to forfeit £5 (equivalent to the value of a cow) for every acre confined. "The townsmen, then, were militantly opposed to any farmer who cared more about his own selfish aims than he did about the common good."[16]

The New England commons existed as a set of shared use-rights to otherwise scarce resources such as crop and meadow lands, pasture, and woodlots. These use-rights were originally held jointly by the town's proprietors, those individuals who had themselves been granted the right to develop and populate a settlement on a specified parcel of land by the general courts of both the Plymouth Colony and its successor, the Massachusetts Bay Colony.[17] These "founding fathers"—they were exclusively male—granted themselves use-rights to the commons that could be bequeathed to heirs or sold as property to non-proprietors, mostly newcomers who were not otherwise entitled to use the common meadows, woodlots, and pastures. Proprietors, and those late-comers who were able to acquire a proprietary interest in the commonage, also took shared responsibility for investing both labor and capital as needed to maintain and develop these common properties. Use-rights to the commons limited the number of trees that could be harvested from the woodlot, the number of cattle and sheep each proprietor could graze on the common pasture, and the amount of grass that could be taken from the meadows.

By pooling labor and capital, the commons allowed those with a proprietary interest to realize certain scale economies that would not otherwise exist on the individual plots of land that one family could reasonably manage. As people working together to fence a pasture, mow and clear a meadow, or manure a field can manage a larger space than can one person working alone with his or her own implements, the commons allowed for a more efficient way to apply

16. Powell, *Puritan Village*, 95.
17. Walcott, "Husbandry in Colonial New England," 221.

productive inputs to land than would have been realized under a more individualized property system. Sumner Powell notes that among Sudbury's original fifty families, only a third owned their own plow shares and pairs of oxen at the time of their deaths.[18] Similar economies of scale are noted by Brian Donahue in reference to Concord's Great Field. Donahue calculates that "Fencing the two-square-mile Great Field required about two thousand rods of fence. Fencing the same area into rectangular eight-acre lots (about the average size of the private lots) would have required over ten thousand rods of fence, or five times as much."[19] Bettye Hobbs Pruitt's analysis of probate court data reveals that as late as the mid-eighteenth century, half of Massachusetts farms lacked both plows and oxen.[20] The commons created scale-economies that freed New Englanders to invest a proportionately greater amount of their wealth in land and consumer durables than their fellow colonists in the middle colonies.[21] While producer durables represented 19 percent of the private physical wealth in middle-colony estates probated in 1774, these same items contributed to only 12 percent of New Englanders' estates in the same year.[22] Meanwhile, land holdings by New Englanders contributed to 70 percent of their wealth, as compared to 63 percent of the wealth of middle colony estates.[23] The "shared-economy" of the twenty-first century was alive and thriving in New England three centuries ago.

The low-input agriculture practiced under the open-field system had a leveling effect on incomes. In 1774, mean household income in New England was $278, while the mean across all thirteen colonies was $345, a difference of over 25 percent.[24] While poorer,

---

18. Walcott, "Husbandry in Colonial New England," 81.

19. Donahue, *Meadow*, 277.

20. Pruitt, "Self-Sufficiency and the Agricultural Economy of Eighteenth-Century Massachusetts," 335.

21. Jones, "Wealth Estimates for the New England Colonies about 1770."

22. Jones, "Wealth Estimates for the New England Colonies," 108.

23. Jones, "Wealth Estimates for the New England Colonies," 108.

24. Lindert and Williamson, "American Colonial Incomes, 1650 to 1774," 37. Income is measured assuming $4.44 per £ sterling.

however, income was more evenly distributed across households in New England. The highest earning 10 percent of New England households in 1774 took home 20 percent of total household income, while the top 10 percent of households in the middle and southern colonies controlled 28.3 percent and 34.3 percent of the income. The middle class—those households receiving between 40 and 80 percent of the income generated—was much stronger in the New England colonies, where they earned 52.5 percent of the income generated in 1774, in contrast with only 40.1 percent and 39.4 percent in the middle and southern colonies, respectively.[25]

Wealth followed a similar pattern. The average wealth of a free adult living in New England in 1774 is estimated at £157 sterling, as compared with £189 sterling for a free adult residing in the middle Colonies.[26] Furthermore, as would be expected in a comparison between self- or village-sufficient economies and market-dependent economies, New England farmers left estates with markedly less material wealth than their compatriots in the other colonies. Indeed, in 1774, it took the assets of two and one half New Englanders to equal the assets of the average southern free wealth holder.[27] Constrained in their ability to supply goods to the economy, colonial New England settlers were equally constrained in their ability to purchase goods from the same economy. Self-sufficiency might have provided sustenance and satisfaction, but it failed to generate much income or material wealth.

Low incomes and self-sufficiency were intertwined. New England's households satisfied about three-quarters of their household demand for goods and services by their own production or by local exchange, which was usually in the form of barter.[28] Payment, in the form of services rendered or material good provided, was often delayed until the service or the good was needed, resulting in "perpetual, complex webs of credit and debt throughout the

25. Lindert and Williamson, "American Colonial Incomes, 1650 to 1774," 37.

26. Jones, "Wealth Estimates for the New England Colonies," 103.

27. Jones, "Wealth and Growth of the Thirteen Colonies," 250.

28. Clark, *The Roots of Rural Capitalism*, 28.

countryside that linked households to one another," creating "networks of obligation alongside those already created by kinship or neighborhood."[29]

Lacking a staple export crop, imports to the region were purchased with income earned through the sale of surpluses from the subsistence-based agriculture that characterized the region. Trade was used to purchase necessities unobtainable locally, or luxuries such as liquor, tea, sugar, and dry goods.

The scale economies realized by the commons system as concerns the use of productive inputs were offset, in large part, by the commons' tremendous administrative costs. Use of the commons was regulated by a body of law, enacted through town ordinances, which were enforced and controlled by elected town selectmen or their designates. Ordinances came into being by agreed-upon voting procedures at town meetings, which occurred as often as once per week. Ordinances specifically relating to the commons governed fencing and fence maintenance, limited grazing rights, regulated water diversion activities, controlled what crops could be raised and when, and set timber harvesting limits.[30] The town council of Braintree, MA, considered the matter of the removal of stones from its commons over one hundred times between 1709 and 1766.[31]

While no doubt tedious and costly to administer, the very existence of the commons demanded the development and maintenance of a significant bureaucracy, and encouraged among town residents habits of cooperation and deliberative, democratic reflection that would in turn aid in regional development. For example, the very same bureaucracy that was developed to regulate the use and maintenance of the commons eventually extended its reach to regulate highway maintenance and construction. Town residents were compelled to supply not only their own labor, but also their teams of oxen for road repair and construction. The commons encouraged investment in social goods such as public safety, roads, public education, and other community-enhancing infrastructure

29. Clark, *The Roots of Rural Capitalism*, 33.

30. MacLear, *Early New England Towns*, 81.

31. *Records of the Town of Braintree, 1640 to 1793.*

whose benefits are not easily appropriated by individual investors. It is fair to say that the rapid industrialization experienced in New England in the early nineteenth century, which far outpaced that experienced in the former middle and southern colonies, is a direct result of the social and economic infrastructure created by two centuries of living in community, surrounded by commons.

Colonial New England's commons proved to be a mixed bag of benefits and costs. On the one hand, the practice of the commons allowed residents of towns and villages across New England access to a means of sustainable self-sufficiency within a defined community. On the other hand, maintenance of the commons required both individual, uncompensated contributions to its overall maintenance, and a generous amount of compromise, none of which would be demanded under a system of exclusive private property, realized under a seemingly unbounded frontier within a political and social environment intent on celebrating the freedom of the individual. The carefully platted, carefully regulated New England commons could not compete with the unbounded physical and political frontiers of the post-revolutionary United States of America. Little by little, individual commitments to the common good were eroded, giving way to a convenient understanding that the common good is achieved by freeing individuals to pursue their own individual ends. This gradual erosion in the commitment to the common good signaled the end of New England's colonial commons and redefined its agrarian commitments. This the topic of our next chapter.

Chapter Three

## Threats to Colonial New England's Commons and Its Agrarianism

We the Subscribers the Committee appointed to consider and report what method appears most advantageous to the Town relative to the disposal of the South Commons beg leave to report that having considered that Subject as thoughroughly as we were able it appears to us that the Town would reap very considerable advantages in the alleviation of their Taxes and the removal of jealousies and animosities by proceeding to appoint and impower a Committee to make sale of the whole of said South Commons.

—Report of the Braintree Town
Committee for the Sale of the South
Common Braintree, April 12th, 1762[1]

ON MARCH 5, 1765, the freeholders and other inhabitants of the town of Braintree, Massachusetts voted "that the North Commons be sold as soon as conveniently," and that a committee, consisting

1. *Records of the Town of Braintree, 1640 to 1793*, 384.

of Mr. John Adams, Samuel Niles, Esq., and Mr. Jonathan Bass[2] "proceed as the season will permit to divide and lay out the North Commons into lots suitable for sale, taking care as far as possible, that there be sufficient springs of water in each."[3]

With this action, the Braintree Commons—1,800 acres of meadow, pasture, and woodlands occupying nearly 20 percent of the town's original area—ceased being property held in common and instead became real estate the city could sell in small, private lots to an ever-growing population. The commons had existed as an essential part of Braintree for over one hundred years, since its incorporation in 1640. Town meetings and town resources had been invested in maintaining its meadows, building access roads, removing illegally erected enclosures, and selectively grooming its forest. Despite the tremendous public and private investment in maintaining this asset, Braintree decided to join an increasing number of other New England towns in transitioning from a land-allocation system that included both private and common property to one in which property in land was exclusively private. This chapter explores those factors that led the voters of Braintree and other colonial New England towns to abandon their commons, leaving concerns over the just allocation of the means of survival to private markets, private charity, and private means.

The fact that more than two hundred years separate privatization decisions adopted by towns of roughly the same age, existing within one hundred miles of each other, originally incorporated as political entities in the same British colony and remaining as political entities in the same commonwealth of the same independent country, argues that a constellation of circumstances, and not some single epiphany or historical event, informed a town's decision to privatize its commons. While Watertown, Massachusetts,

---

2. This was John Adams' entrance into public life. In thirty-two years, he would become the second president of the United States. Samuel Niles, Adams' friend, legal advisor, and neighbor, was the son and namesake of the 2nd Congregational Church of Braintree, MA. Jonathan Bass was a fellow resident of Braintree, and a descendent of Deacon Samuel Bass, who arrived in Braintree in 1640.

3. *Records of the Town of Braintree, 1640 to 1793*, 400.

privatized its common fields in 1680, the citizens of Sandwich, Massachusetts, shared common lands and fencing through at least 1888.[4] The western Massachusetts towns of Northampton and Deerfield were founded within twenty-four years of each other (1653 and 1677, respectively) and are separated by only sixteen miles, but while Northampton privatized its commons in 1753, Deerfield maintained its common fields until 1858.[5] The publicly owned "Great Meadow" in Hadley, Massachusetts (founded in 1659), exists to this day (managed by the city itself), and is recognized as a World Monument by the World Monuments Fund.[6]

Free-market-loving political pundits writing for the popular press celebrate Plymouth Colony's 1623 decision to allow families a property right in their own corn production as a triumph of liberal economic thought over ill-advised attempts to force the pursuit of the common good. These narratives (often published around Thanksgiving), serve as "just-so" stories; myths that instruct, caution, and inform. Michael Franc, a former Distinguished Fellow at the Heritage Foundation, argues in an article published on the foundation's website in November 2005, that the "pilgrims beat 'communism' with the free market," due to their "courageous decision to embrace the free-market principle of private property ownership."[7] Jerry Bowyer writes in a November 2008 article in *Forbes* that the first Thanksgiving "was a celebration of abundance after a period of socialism and starvation," adding that as a result of what they had learned during the dark days of socialism, "the colonists threw off the statist intellectual fashions of their day. They concluded that the ancient principles of private property as recorded in the Ten Commandments were superior to

4. Field and Kimball, "Managing Common-Property Resources," 13; Libby, "Early History of the Fence," 401.

5. Field and Kimball, "Managing Common-Property Resources," 36–37.

6. https://www.wmf.org/project/cultural-landscape-hadley-massachusetts. Accessed 11/5/2021.

7. https://www.heritage.org/markets-and-finance/commentary/pilgrims-beat-communism-free-market. Accessed 11/4/2021.

the utopian speculations of Plato and his 17th-century imitators."[8] An unattributed author at the Cascade Policy Institute writes in November 2012 that Governor Bradford "learned at Plymouth's first Thanksgiving" that "instituting private property and a market economy . . . caused Plymouth to survive."[9] Right-wing pundits have used Thanksgiving as a context to argue for the ineluctable supremacy of private property rights and free-market economies.

Aside from ignoring the fact that common fields and meadows continued to proliferate across the towns established in both the Plymouth and Massachusetts Bay Colonies for a hundred years after Bradford's 1623 decision, the authors of these triumphal articles—and they are legion—have their facts wrong. To begin with, the "first thanksgiving" was held in 1621, two years *prior* to Bradford's decision to allow private claims to the corn grown and harvested as a result of individual efforts. The "period of socialism" was in full swing at the time the Pilgrims joined with their Native American neighbors to celebrate a feast of thanksgiving. The Pilgrims and their "socialist" practices survived—by hard work, luck, and perhaps providence—for more than two years after this first thanksgiving. In 1623, as survival was more assured, the focus switched to promoting surpluses, and the Pilgrims adopted a policy of giving a property right to the *output* of labor applied to the land, but *not to the land itself.* That is, contrary to the statements made in these articles, Bradford's 1623 decision did not institute private property in land, nor did it open up the small, isolated colony at Plymouth to a market economy; there were no markets in Plymouth. Bradford's 1623 decision simply allowed Plymouth's residents to a claim of private property in the corn they grew.

Bradford's decision to allow private claims to the fruit of human labor is best viewed in a Lockean way; labor creates the title

---

8. https://www.forbes.com/2008/11/27/thanksgiving-economy-history-oped-cx_jb_1127bowyer.html?sh=671d1523460a. Accessed 11/4/21.

9. "What Governor Bradford Learned at Plymouth's First Thanksgiving." https://cascadepolicy.org/economic-opportunity/what-governor-bradford-learned-at-plymouths-first-thanksgiving/. Accessed 11/4/2021.

of property.[10] This was the lesson learned by the original settlers in Plymouth Bay. Cropland, meadow, pasture, and forest—which existed without labor's effort, whose God-given existence provided the means to survival to all within a community—was *still commonly owned* within the Plymouth colony as a matter of giving all a God-given and just right to the resources needed for survival.

However, while Plymouth and hundreds of other New England towns founded in the seventeenth and early eighteenth centuries utilized a shared field system and commons, this practice was eventually abandoned. This was not in any way a result of some colony-wide conversion to a free-market ideology. Rather, three factors—population growth, the introduction of a cash-based, market economy, and a lack of political support for the commons among the second and third generations of New England's settlers—gradually forced New England's commoners to abandon the common field system and the agrarian practices of low-input, sustainable farming that it fostered.

Changes brought about by increases in population exerted profound effects on the relationship between a town's residents and its commons. Population growth, unmet by proportionate increases in the incorporated land mass, resulted in an ever-growing number of landless town residents, many of whom were the sons and grandsons of the towns' founders. Within ten years of its incorporation in 1639, at least twenty-two adult sons of Sudbury, Massachusetts' founders were landless men, basically living at the parental home and farming the parental fields.[11] This extended filial dependence was met, throughout New England, not only by emigration to newly established towns on the western and northern borders, but also with a remarkable increase in premarital pregnancies. During the second half of the seventeenth century, the percentage of recorded births in Massachusetts occurring within the first eight months of marriage increased by nearly a factor of three, from 9 percent of recorded first births to 26 percent.[12] James

10. Locke, *Second Treatise*, 121.

11. Powell, *Puritan Village*, 118.

12. Smith and Hindus, "Premarital Pregnancy in America 1640–1971."

Henretta suggests, not too subtlety, that particularly within a culture that shunned out-of-wedlock births, premarital pregnancies became a useful way of obtaining land rights from parents otherwise reluctant to surrender control of some of their landholdings.[13]

So long as they continued living in the town of their birth, not even a parent's death would be able to change the landless condition of many of the sons of the original settlers. The platted boundaries of the commons allowed no mechanism for a family to bequeath more than one share in the commons to (one member of) the next generation. Commoners wishing to support all of their children upon their deaths were forced to cash in their common-right, thus providing a financial—as opposed to a physical—estate to their multiple heirs, who needed money to start new farms in new settlements. As an increasing number of commoners relinquished their common-right, the legal status of the commons changed from joint ownership, or common property, to several ownership, or private property.

Increasing population exerted pressure on even private lands, as individual plots shrank as they were increasingly divided among sons and grandsons. According to historian Christopher Clark, by the end of the eighteenth century, farmsteads in Northampton had so dwindled in size that less than 20 percent of Northampton farmers had holdings sufficiently large to divide among their sons; only one child could inherit the average-sized Northampton farmstead.[14] Population pressures no doubt help to explain the 103 year difference between Northampton's and Deerfield's decisions to privatize their common fields and pastures. In 1765, Northampton's population was 1,628, while nearby Deerfield had a population of only 737.[15] As both towns occupied roughly the same area, Northampton's significantly greater population density no doubt increased the incentive to privatize its commons to increase the

13. Henretta, "Families and Farms," 31.

14. Clark, *The Roots of Rural Capitalism*, 62.

15. Greene and Harrington, *American Population before the Federal Census of 1790*, 26–27.

land mass available to those citizens willing and able to pay for the property right.

As land in Massachusetts Bay Colony became more scarce and therefore more costly, an increasingly smaller percentage of its inhabitants were able to pursue a farming career: The "entry barriers" to this profession became increasingly difficult to surmount. Late eighteenth-century arrivals to Northampton had merchandise valued in excess of £100, with only £1 worth of property, and with no tillage or other improved land.[16] New England's colonial residents gradually acquired other skills by which they could earn a living separately from farming. This latter strategy gave rise to new manufacturing activities that served as the forerunners of the "capitalist industrial revolution" that was to take place in New England.[17]

This increase in cottage-level manufacturing activity—originally undertaken so as to augment farm income and purchase imports such as spices, sugar, tea, coffee, rum, and raisins—accelerated as a result of the post-war credit crisis brought about by New England's mounting trade deficit with England. By 1784, exports to England from the former New England colonies were only a tenth of the value of British imports to the New England. As a result of this trade deficit, English exporters began to demand cash (specie) from their New England wholesale importers, who in turn pressured their local merchants for cash in place of farm commodities. At the local level, this meant that the country store would no longer accept farm produce in lieu of cash. The abrupt, post-war change to a cash-based economy forced many of New England's self-sufficient but cash-poor farmers to sell land and livestock to meet the debts accumulated while they were serving in the colonial military. This "chain of debt" fomented the unrest that led to Shays' Rebellion, and hastened the conversion of New England's self-sufficient, sustainable, agrarian economy to a more mercantile, commercially based economy.[18] A manufacturing

16. Nobles, "The Rise of Merchants in Rural Market Towns," 11.
17. Clark, *The Roots of Rural Capitalism*, 64.
18. Szatmary, *Shays' Rebellion*.

economy, such as what started to take hold in New England in the mid-nineteenth century, had no need for a common field system.

As the population of each town grew relative to the number of the original founders, the justice, or fairness, of the land allocation that relied on the commons became increasingly questioned, resulting in decreased popular support for the institution. As described by Nobel laureate Elinor Ostrom in her research on the commons, for a commons itself to be sustainable—that is, for a commons itself to continue to provide the services for which it was originally created—the common lands and resources need to have clear and enforceable limits, not only on their own, physical boundaries, and but on who is allowed to exercise use-rights to these commons.[19] In colonial New England, both the physical boundaries of the commons and the use-rights to common meadows, forests, cropland, and pasture were established at the time of the town's incorporation, and typically distributed in proportion to the magnitude of the investment an individual, known as a proprietor, had committed to the town at its founding. These investment opportunities were themselves limited to "freemen", white males who were members in good standing of an existing Puritan church who had taken an oath pledging loyalty and duty to the colonial government. Potential proprietors petitioning the general court for a land grant needed to show the court that among them, they had the means to develop a successful new town in the New England wilderness. This in turn meant that, among them, they had the collective means to pay to have the land surveyed and platted, to pay to secure title to the land from the Native American tribe or tribes occupying the area, to build access roads to and within the town, and to call a pastor and pay for his salary and dwelling, and to pay for the fees of the general court. These town founders platted townships that included commons in pasture, meadow, forest, and cropland for their use. They could sell these use-rights to newcomers; they could bequeath them to an heir, rent them to others, or use them as their own, provided that their use of the commons did not impair or obstruct the use

19. Ostrom, *Governing the Commons*, 90.

of other "commoners." Newcomers to the town, which together with the proprietors constituted the group known as inhabitants, could receive land grants to private property, but typically not to the commons; these rights would have to be purchased or rented from the proprietors under the Lockean conditions that use would result in "as good and as much" for the rest of the commoners. The joint ownership and management control of the common lands rested, at the time of settlement, exclusively with the proprietors; non-commoners—of which, with the exception of women and children, few existed when the town was first incorporated—had no say in the management of the commons.

This exclusionary principle, key to the survivability of the commons, proved to be a Gordian knot for those same proprietors whose survival depended directly on attracting new members to the settlements. Who would leave family and home and travel across an ocean to be forever a second-class resident of a wild and dangerous country? Who could look at his neighbor in Christian love, and not feel pulled to grant the neighbor the same rights as he enjoyed? Perhaps to attract more people to these sparsely populated chartered towns, or perhaps to keep peace and cultivate community bonds within these frontier establishments, or perhaps to reflect the radical leveling that is at the core of the Christian gospel, or perhaps some combination of all of the above, the exclusionary principle of limiting decision-making control of the commons was abandoned quickly—first by lack of enforcement, and later by decree of the General Court.[20] By 1641, the Massachusetts Body of Liberties, commissioned by and submitted to the General Court of the Massachusetts Bay Colony as a guide to the colony's future statutes included, as Liberty 12, a right of participation in governance to "every man whether Inhabitant or forreiner, free or not free." This same section granted each of these individuals "libertie to come to any publique Court, Councel, or Towne meeting, and either by speech or writeing to move any lawfull, seasonable, and materiall question, or to present any necessary motion, complaint, petition, Bill or information, whereof that meeting hath proper

20. Brown, "Freemanship in Puritan Massachusetts," 870.

cognizance, so it be done in convenient time, due order, and respective manner."[21] With this liberty, the Gordian knot was cut—all white male inhabitants had at least a voice, and in many towns, a vote, in the management of the commons. However, in releasing the bonds of this knot, the exclusionary principle that supported the commons was undermined. As control of the commons passed to an ever larger and diverse group of people, town meetings across New England grew increasingly heated as non-commoners chafed at restrictions imposed on the use of these properties. Management of the commons became increasingly contentious and confused, and the commons themselves suffered from neglect and unlawful incursions. John Adams, writing about Braintree's commons and their 1765 sale, notes that Braintree's shared fields "in their common Situation, they appeared to me of very little Utility to the Public or to Individuals: Under the care of Proprietors . . . they would probably be better managed. And more productive."[22]

Whether the Body of Liberties catalyzed even wider participation by non-commoners in the management of the commons or simply reflected an already accepted practice of broader participation in town governance than that which was officially encoded in the laws of the existing town theocracy is impossible to determine with certainty, and will remain a matter for debate among historians. What is clear to us is that, as town populations became both larger and more diverse—as reflected in the decreased percentage of inhabitants with membership in the town's Puritan church—participation in the governance and use of the commons was expanded to include an ever greater number of town residents, many of whom lacked status as freemen. Eventually, proprietors and commoners were outnumbered at town meetings by neighbors who had no permanent claim to the common resource. As land values across the settled parts of New England increased, and as

21. *The Massachusetts Body of Liberties*, 1641. https://history.hanover.edu/texts/masslib.html. Accessed 11/15/21.

22. John Adams autobiography, part 1, "John Adams," through 1776, sheet 8 of 53 [electronic edition]. *Adams Family Papers: An Electronic Archive*. Massachusetts Historical Society. http://www.masshist.org/digitaladams/. Accessed 11/16/2021.

town taxes and needs increased, and as the ability of the commons to provide a subsistence standard of living for all decreased, retaining the land as commons became an increasingly costly decision, particularly in light of the benefits this same land could provide the town coffers were it to be platted and sold. Braintree's 1765 decision to sell off its commons was one among hundreds of such decisions made over a two-hundred-year period in colonial and post-colonial New England. It reflected the region's reluctant but increasing reliance on markets and money as the means of providing access to life's necessities. Those interested in pursuing farming as a means of supporting themselves and their multigenerational families moved to less settled areas in northwestern Massachusetts, Connecticut, Vermont, and Maine where, with ecclesiastical authority exerting an ever dwindling influence, they could farm on plots of land so large as to make the commons unnecessary.[23]

While population pressure, the need for greater participation in an ever-expanding market economy, and a growing sense that neither hereditary privilege nor loyalty oaths to some ecclesiastical authority were necessary for a just distribution of land and its bounty (and in fact, popular opinion increasingly questioned the justice of these arrangements) eventually caused towns across New England to sell their common lands, the commons continued exert a beneficial influence on the practices and perspectives of New England's inhabitants.

New England's commons-based agrarian system produced enduring results—not only by inculcating social habits as skills promoting citizenship and cooperation, but also by developing among the residents habits of land stewardship that reflected and responded to the productive limits of the land itself. The 1879 census of agriculture, which was the first to report per-acre yields by state and county, records that after two-and-a-half centuries of cultivation, New England's farmlands exceeded national averages in their per-acre yields of corn, oats, wheat, barley, and buckwheat.[24] Meanwhile, as early as 1820, the amount of exhausted and abandoned

23. Tracey, "Re-Considering Migration within Colonial New England."
24. Bell, "Did New England Go Downhill?" 457.

farm land in North Carolina exceeded the amount of land in cultivation.[25] In 1819, George Washington Jeffreys, a minister of the Methodist Episcopal church and the corresponding secretary of the Agricultural Society of North Carolina, chastised North Carolina farmers for their "land-killing system" of agriculture, which, "must ultimately issue in want, misery, and depopulation."[26] New England and the South continued their divergent farming practices—one of stewardship and the other of plunder—into the twentieth century. By 1936, while New England continued to enjoy remarkably stable yields from its agricultural lands, the Southern Regional Committee of the Social Science Research Council concluded that the vast majority of the nation's eroded land (61 percent, or 91.5 million acres, to be precise), existed in the South.[27] Rooted in the commons, New England's agrarian system succeeded in establishing an as-yet-unrivaled form of sustainable agriculture.

We argue that these results are not accidental. Two characteristics unique to the commons and essential to its very manifestation were arguably responsible to its enduring success as a policy encouraging land stewardship. First, as conceived and as realized throughout its history, the commons shaped communities in which inhabitants were constantly confronted with evidence of their own interdependence and the physical limitations of the resource base that supported them. If a person failed to maintain his portion of a fence, another person's cattle could easily escape. If one person harvested too much wood, others would lack what they needed for construction and fuel. *The commons provided a framework for understanding the role of individual actions in a resource-dependent life shared in community.* As a result of the organizing framework necessitated by the commons, other natural resources existing within the boundaries of the New England village were allocated by joint consent of those granted franchise. The village of Sudbury employed "timber keepers" whose job it was

25. Cathey, "Sidney Weller," 5.

26. Jeffreys, (pseud. Agricola), *A Series of Essays on Agriculture and Rural Affairs in Forty-Seven Numbers*, 5.

27. Stoll, *Larding the Lean Earth*, 138.

to assure that "all timber be befallen to any man's necessity."[28] In Concord, rights not only to the common meadow but also to "cut wood and timber, and to dig sand, clay, and gravel" were subject to community-endorsed regulation.[29] The New England commons provided a successful way for humankind to respond to the challenge, noted by Wes Jackson, to "live within the means, [and] not exceed the natural recharge rate of the forces at work on the earth's crust."[30] The modest, sustainable life of the common-field New England town allowed families to flourish without importing carrying capacity. As there was nowhere else to go to substitute for what their own stewardship destroyed, the inhabitants of the New England towns of the seventeenth and eighteenth centuries were careful to avoid destruction.[31]

Historian Brian Donahue argues that "the ecological limits that bounded such local economies were demolished by the market revolution," which "drove a more extensive, exploitative approach to farming" that included a "spectacular burst in land clearing" in the second quarter of the nineteenth century. However, we beg for a more nuanced understanding that blames not the market, per se, but the decision to change common-property resources—particularly to land productivity and forest health that had been a source of community wealth—to unprotected open-access resources to be appropriated and squandered by whoever had a property right to the land itself.[32] That is, so long cropland, meadow, pastures, and forests were held in common as part of New England's agrarian tradition, each commoner was obliged to consider the effects of his land-use practices on the other commoners. Once the commons were privatized, individual autonomous landowners were allowed greater freedom in their use of "their" private property, which was, by default, expanded to include the health of the soils, pasture,

28. Quoted by Powell, *Puritan Village*, 96.

29. Donahue, *The Great Meadow*, 86.

30. Jackson, *Consulting the Genius of the Place*, 68.

31. Rasmussen, *Faith*, 195.

32. Donahue, "Environmental Stewardship and Decline in Old New England," 239.

and forests found within these newly platted and purchased, private boundaries. While some of these new private property owners clearly decided to follow the practices of land and forest stewardship that they inherited from their predecessors, others succumbed to the temptation to use more exploitative practices in order to increase their private profits. That this temptation arose is not so much the fault of the market economy, but the fault of a belief that voluntary market transactions reflect *just* exchanges between private individuals who bear the entire costs of their decisions, a belief that until the latter half of the twentieth century went largely unquestioned. As it became increasingly obvious that our private production and consumption activities affect our present and future neighbors, the justice of the private exchanges, in the face of clearly *incomplete* markets, is increasingly challenged.[33]

The justice of the commons forced New Englanders to recognize the *interrelatedness* of their actions and thereby encouraged *greater stewardship* of environmental resources, but the same commons' necessary exclusivity appeared to be (and was) increasingly unjust in the face of increases in population and religious diversity. The justice of a market economy that replaced the commons stresses voluntary trades among free individuals, regardless of religious affiliation and practice, patrimony, or first occupancy. However, to the extent that markets are incomplete, a free market economy results in injustice when participants are allowed to ignore the impact of their actions on present and future generations.

With the demise of the commons and the subsequent shift from communitarianism to individualism, the nature of social and political questions confronting New Englanders experienced a parallel shift. Issues in civic ethics and morality began to revolve around the development of the best individuals rather than the best communities. In his essay, "Private Property and Common Wealth," Wendell Berry appears to ignore the successful, two-hundred-year-old history of the highly regulated New England commons when he writes that, "You cannot get good care in the

33. An incomplete market is one that fails to reflect *all* the costs and benefits a market exchange imposes.

use of the land by demanding it from public officials. . . . No mere law, divine or human, could conceivably be enough to protect the land while we are using it."[34] But Berry is wrong, and unnecessarily polarizing. As proof, human and divine law combined for over two hundred years in the form of the shared, and sustainable common fields of New England.

Berry's beliefs are in many ways consistent with those of the original Twelve Southerners, who responded to perceived market injustices with an anti-industry screed that blamed "industrialism" for everything from unemployment to income inequality, to the loss of religion, manners, and conversation.[35] Modern day heirs to the anti-industrial agrarian impulse of the Twelve Southerners focus on controlling markets, rather than human behavior. Wendell Berry has called for production controls and price supports "for every product of farming and forestry," but stops short of endorsing any direct governmental constraints on the behavior of farmers themselves.[36] Berry's reticence to endorse government regulation of farming practices has been disappointing. Berry and other followers of the Jeffersonian agrarian tradition appear eager to blame factors outside of a farmer's control—prices, interest rates, bank loan policies—for creating dead zones in the Gulf of Mexico, endangering native species, or depleting and polluting ground and surface waters. Following Jefferson's assertion that farmers were "God's chosen people," in whose breasts God deposited "substantial and genuine virtue," it is unfortunate, but not surprising that Jefferson's intellectual heirs have argued for regulation of everything except the behavior of the farmers themselves.

The Jeffersonian agrarians have advocated a naively informed, poorly argued Manichaean philosophy that labels all things industrial as bad, and all farmers (except for the industrial ones, whoever they are) as good. We find this view both uninformed

---

34. Berry, *Another Turn of the Crank*.

35. The Twelve Southerners, *I'll Take my Stand*, xlv–vlvii.

36. Wendell Berry, as quoted in Olmstead, "Wendell Berry's Right Kind of Farming." https://www.nytimes.com/2018/10/01/opinion/wendell-berry-agriculture-farm-bill.html. Accessed 11/20/2021.

by history and in conflict with church teachings on vocation. The New England commons provided a sustainable way to farm the same land for hundreds of years, even as industrial development continued, hand in glove, across the colony and, eventually, its states and commonwealths. The Southern "headright" system of individual, private landholdings does not have the same record. And, to our knowledge, God has favored no vocation.

Nonetheless, the beauty of Jefferson's tribute continues to convince many people today of the superiority of the free, unregulated yeoman farmer. This romantic view is held atavistically among some of us whose ancestors left the farm generations ago, romantically among some of us who find no farmers in our heritage but love the land, and inspirationally among the young who hope for a better, more unified way of linking a clear need for provisioning with a love of the earth and its limited resources. But the simple truth is that farmers are not better than the rest of us, and one enduring legacy of New England's commons is that the Puritan settlers recognized this. Sin is, at its core, self-centered, self-regarding behavior that fails to honor God and neighbor. New England's commons regulated and constrained this behavior, forcing each individual to regard explicitly the welfare of the neighbor.

For at least two hundred years following the arrival of the Pilgrims at Plymouth, New England's colonies—and eventually its states and commonwealths—practiced a form of land distribution and land-use regulation that recognized, as a matter of both justice and survival, the common interests of all inhabitants in the health of a community's forested, pastured, and crop lands. This practice was slowly abandoned and replaced by a reliance on private property rights, coupled with freedom to pursue one's economic interest in private markets. Two hundred years later, it seems time to examine how the lessons in sustainability learned from New England's experiment with the commons might contribute to the informing agricultural policy today. This is the topic of our final chapter.

Chapter Four

_____

# A New England Agrarianism for Today

If any proprietor in any common or general field shal put, or
cause to be put therein any horse, cattle sheep, or other creature,
over and above the number allowed him, or before the day agreed
upon; or keep them longer there than the time set and limited by
a major vote of the proprietors, he shall be deemed a trespasser;
and his creaturs so put in shall be proceeded with by any of the
proprietors as creatures taken damage saisant, to all intents and
purposes, as much as if he owned no land within such general field.

—The Perpetual Laws of the
Commonwealth of Massachusetts[1]

1. An ACT concerning general and common fields. Section 5. February 24,
1786, in Thomas and Andrews, *The Perpetual Laws of the Commonwealth of
Massachusetts*, 289. https://books.google.com/books?id=ADw4AAAAIAAJ&
pg=PA291&dq=closure+%22common+fields%22+%22massachusetts%22&hl
=en&newbks=1&newbks_redir=1&sa=X&ved=2ahUKEwjom9Wz8urzAhVy
DzQIHW4SBJoQ6AF6BAgFEAI. Accessed 10/27/2021.

## A New England Agrarianism for Today

There is a straine in a man's heart that will sometime or other runne out to excesse, unlesse the Lord restraine it, but it is not good to venture it: It is necessary therefore, that all power that is on earth be limited, Church-power or other: If there be power given to speak great things, then look for great blasphemies, look for a licentious abuse of it. It is counted a matter of danger to the State to limit Prerogatives; but it is a further danger, not to have them limited.

—John Cotton, 1656[2]

Nothing can take form except within limits. No cure is possible, either in policy or practice, except within understood limits.

—Wendell Berry, 2018[3]

COLONIAL NEW ENGLAND'S AGRARIANISM was founded on the paired beliefs that our survival depends on our abilities to live cooperatively and within prescribed limits. These two beliefs were manifest in a system of land distribution, tenure, and stewardship that imposed constraints on individual liberty in order to achieve the necessary cooperation and observance of limits.

These beliefs, and the common field system that they inspired, went largely unchallenged for the first two hundred years of European settlement in New England, despite the fact that cooperation proved difficult and costly, and settlers and their fortunes were frequently tested by the agreed-upon limits. Eventually, the opportunities provided to white settlers in the early nineteenth century to inhabit an apparently limitless western frontier, coupled with an as-yet-unsurpassed period of technological innovation and industrialization, successfully challenged beliefs in the necessity of cooperation and limits. Over the next two hundred years, beliefs

2. Cotton, *An Exposition upon the Thirteenth Chapter of the Revelation*, 73. http://name.umdl.umich.edu/A34679.0001.001. Accessed 12/22/21.

3. Olmstead, "Opinion: Wendell Berry's Right Kind of Farming." https://www.nytimes.com/2018/10/01/opinion/wendell-berry-agriculture-farm-bill.html. Accessed 12/21/2021.

in the superiority a society founded on individual autonomy and individual freedom supplanted social commitments to cooperation and constraints.

Today, however, four hundred years after the first commons were cleared, fenced, and managed by the Pilgrims in Plymouth, and two hundred years after the commons were replaced by privatized lands, we find that once again our very survival as a resource-dependent species depends on developing means of cooperating and living within limits that honor the capacities of the resources on which we depend. New England's agrarian expression provides a useful model to apply to challenges faced today, not only in agriculture, but as encountered by such seemingly intractable problems as climate change, aquifer depletion, air pollution, and a host of other environmental problems. This chapter considers how early New England's agrarianism can enlighten and inform contemporary United States farm policy, and offers a modest proposal for a set of "first steps" that might help us begin to work cooperatively to live within the constraints that earth's resource systems require.

## Agricultural Regulation in the Post-Commons World: The Triumph of Jeffersonian Agrarianism

Perhaps because the privatization of the commons took place synchronously with the expansion of the U.S. frontier, questions of resource scarcity and exhaustibility did not enter the discussion as colonial New England's town boards considered whether or not to privatize common lands. And perhaps because, when the U.S. Constitution was ratified in 1788, the federal government had more urgent questions before it than those presented by land-use practices among farmers, no one seemed to question the lack of any nationally expressed concern that critical resources—land, water, and air—be managed in a way that left as much and as good for other citizens. Instead, the entire question of who—if anyone—was responsible for the coordinated management of natural resources was left up to individual states. And perhaps because these new states had more urgent questions, and perhaps because the "takings clause" in the fifth amendment to the Constitution made government regulation of activities on private property potentially costly for the regulators, no one in the early days of this nation seemed to question each state's lack of concern for the coordinated management of natural resources.[4] The carefully crafted, assiduously enforced, regularly revisited and revised rules governing the New England commons were simply not replaced in the laws of the new nation or the newly created states. Private rights of farmers to the use of the land they owned and air they shared were absolute and conferred with the land's property right. While the Massachusetts Bay Colony adopted the first animal cruelty law in 1641, the statute did not become a part of the laws of the state of Massachusetts. Rather, state-enforced animal protection did not exist in this country until 1828, when New York State enacted an animal cruelty law that made it a misdemeanor to "neglect, maliciously kill, maim, wound, injure, torture or cruelly beat any horse, mule, ox, cattle, sheep, or other animal belonging to himself or another."[5] While all fifty states have enacted similar laws, many states offer exceptions from these laws for agricultural husbandry practices. Water rights alone were conditional and contingent throughout the nation's history. Among the original thirteen states, private use of surface waters was governed by a doctrine of "reasonable use" among those owning property in the riparian zone. Reasonable use is typically interpreted as use that meet the "as much and as good" criterion.

Whatever the reason, the regulatory apparatus developed for the New England commons to promote a form of sustainable resource stewardship and an egalitarian approach to resource access and distribution had little or no influence on the laws of the new nation nor its constituent states. Instead, the privatization of New England's commons brought to an effective end the regulation of agricultural practices in the United States. This is remarkable, not

---

4. This clause reads, "Nor shall private property be taken for public use, without just compensation." This has been used by land owners to demand compensation from government for regulations constraining uses of private property.

5. Quoted in Tannenbaum, "Animals and the Law," 565–66.

only given the enormous subsidies received by the agricultural sector, but also given agriculture's contributions to environmental degradation.[6] Agriculture presently contributes 10 percent of total U.S. greenhouse gas emissions.[7] It is the primary source of impairments to the nation's rivers and streams.[8] Agriculture is second only land development as a source of wetland destruction,[9] and second only to atmospheric deposition as a source of impairment to the nation's lakes, reservoirs, and ponds.[10] All but the largest animal feedlots are allowed to operate without any permit system setting legal limits on the amount of waste allowed to enter surface waters. There is no governmental oversight of land-based pesticide use by the farming sector; farmers as a group may legally apply billions of tons of biological and chemical pesticides to their land without any other requirement than they "follow label instructions."[11] Problems with overspray are handled with case-by-case, common-law trespass suits between neighbors.

Indeed, not only has agriculture avoided most regulation, it is now protected against those activities that threaten to discipline farm practices by exposing particularly egregious actions

6. According to the Environmental Working Group, agricultural subsidies in 2020 total $20 billion. See https://www.ewg.org/interactive-maps/2021-farm-subsidies-ballooned-under-trump/.

7. U.S. Environmental Protection, Agency. *Sources of Greenhouse Gas Emissions*. https://www.epa.gov/ghgemissions/sources-greenhouse-gas-emissions#agriculture. Accessed 12/28/21.

8. U.S. Environmental Protection Agency, Nonpoint Source: Agriculture. https://www.epa.gov/nps/nonpoint-source-agriculture. Accessed 12/23/21.

9. U.S. Environmental Protection Agency, Water Quality Assessment and TMDL Information, National Summary of State Information, 2017. https://ofmpub.epa.gov/waters10/attains_nation_cy.control#WETLAND. Accessed 12/23/21.

10. U.S. Environmental Protection Agency, Water Quality Assessment and TMDL Information, National Summary of State Information, 2017. https://ofmpub.epa.gov/waters10/attains_nation_cy.control#LAKE/RESERVOIR/POND. Accessed 12/23/21.

11. U.S. Environmental Protection Agency, Water Quality Assessment and TMDL Information, National Summary of State Information, 2017. https://ofmpub.epa.gov/waters10/attains_nation_cy.control#LAKE/RESERVOIR/POND. Accessed 12/23/21.

as they take place on the farm. "Ag-gag" bills (also known as *agricultural protection acts*) criminalize the unauthorized recording of farm practices, threatening would-be whistleblowers with fines and imprisonment. While the constitutionality of these laws is still being tested in the courts, for the time being they are the law of the land in Alabama, Arkansas, Iowa, Kansas, Missouri, Montana, North Dakota, and Utah.

The remarkable lack of regulation of the U.S. agricultural sector testifies to the enduring strength of the Jeffersonian agrarian tradition, and its core argument that if farmers are to be virtuous, they must be independent and free. Jeffersonian agrarians—and here we include not only Jefferson himself, but his intellectual heirs, such as Wendell Berry—espouse an agrarianism that is at best suspicious of, and at worst antagonistic to, government, except as a source of subsidies and enforced quotas on production. Following Jefferson's lead, today's agrarians argue that, were farmers free from competition and its resulting low prices, farm practices would become more environmentally benign. Rather than seek to encourage participation in the creation of enforceable policies that would constrain the abuse of the land and the people and animals that rely on it, today's agrarians cultivate a hermeneutic of suspicion regarding government involvement in agriculture, while relying primarily on exhortation to discipline the self-interest that drives the current agrarian crisis. Today's agrarians—wary as they are of government—ignore the government's remarkable success in constraining the environmentally destructive behavior of those industries that have been targeted for regulation.[12] Their silence on these matters deserves some attention and correction.

In contrast to the Jeffersonian agrarians, whose focus has always been on farmers and farming, the New England agrarian

12. A recent study of pollution levels at Louisiana terminus of the Mississippi River show that, since passage of the Clean Air and Clean Water Acts in early 1970s, lead levels in the river are one thousand times lower than they were in 1979, pH has increased from an acidic level of 5.8 to its present level of 8.2, and bacterial levels have been reduced by 99 percentage points. See Turner, "Declining Bacteria, Lead, and Sulphate, and Rising pH and Oxygen in the Lower Mississippi River."

tradition focuses on *the natural resource base itself*. As such, New Englanders constrained the use of the commons so as to promote *its* sustainability, and not—in contrast to the Jeffersonian agrarians—the sustainability of farms and farmers. The New England agrarian tradition also takes a more critical view of liberty's ability to serve as a source of virtue. More than a century before Jefferson wrote his paean to the virtuous and free yeoman farmer, Puritan pastor John Cotton criticized the logical construct that links virtue with liberty. In his *Exposition on the Thirteenth Chapter of Revelation,* Cotton argues that "many a carnall heart will say . . . if he get but liberty, God and men shll see what a new man he will be: O the bottomlesse depth of a deceitfull heart!"[13] The good pastor goes on to offer a prescient critique of the yet-to-be-articulated Jeffersonian agrarian tradition, writing in this same sermon that, "There is no man naturally but he thinks this is his freedom to have his owne minde not crossed, to have his full liberty in the world, to have good bargains, and not to be pinched in this and that, and not for conscience to fly in his face; it is a sign a man is yet a natural born captive."[14] Founded as it was on a belief in humankind's captivity to self-interest and sin, the New England agrarian tradition did not look to liberty or more congenial market outcomes as a means of disciplining human behavior. The New England tradition focuses both blame and corrective action on the individual.

By emphasizing the corruptible nature of the individual, Puritan religion contributed to a society more willing than our present one to regulate individual behavior. While it is common practice today to blame environmental problems on human initiatives and institutions—globalization, the government, the market economy, corporations—the Puritans saw overuse of the commons as the result of selfishness, pride, greed, and other individual failings—our original sin. The Puritans therefore directed regulatory action at the individual, and not at some amorphous, non-human "other" represented as an institution. As the Puritans viewed the individual as the locus of the problem, rather than rely on exhortation and

13. Cotton, *Revelation*, 76.
14. Cotton, *Revelation*, 185.

appeals to virtue, the they relied on democratically imposed and popularly enforced *laws* that constrained individuals to limit their use of the commons.

The agrarian tradition of colonial New England rested on a foundation that explicitly recognized human proclivity to engage in self-regarding behavior to the detriment of our communities and those who come after us. As attested to by the lack of success realized by the agricultural "improvers" of the nineteenth century, mere exhortation cannot be relied upon to provide a sufficient countervailing response to our self-regarding impulses.[15] Rather, these impulses can only be constrained by public policy. The New England town councils, with their no-doubt interminable weekly meetings, provided the necessary constraints to the self-serving individualism that resulted in exhausted soils and depopulated land throughout the rest of the colonies, particularly those of the South. The New England agrarian system of land stewardship lasted for two hundred years because it relied upon, not merely exhortation aimed at converting individuals to a particular worldview, but on forcing both the converted and the non-converted to conform to an enforceable policy of land stewardship which threatened violators severe sanctions, including the loss of property. In doing so, the New England agrarian system put the blame for overuse of the commons squarely on the individual caught in the act of pasturing too many animals, or failing to manure his share of the common cropland, or felling too many trees from the common forest. Unlike today's Jeffersonian agrarians, individuals participating in the New England common field system could not excuse their overuse of the commons by appeals to the caprices of a market economy, or to asymmetries in the distribution of income or wealth, or to the harsh realities of farm life. *Stewardship was not merely an individual virtue; under the New England commons system, it was an enforced community value.*

We need to reclaim the right, exercised by the New England agrarians, to demand that agriculture steward the natural

---

15. Donahue, "Environmental Stewardship and Decline in Old New England," 237.

resource commons as a treasured and critical resource. Exhortation, excuses, and scapegoating markets and governments have, unsurprisingly, proven to be ineffective tools in achieving this end. Equally ineffective are pie-in-the-sky proposals that require massive changes in the way things are, such as proposals to limit control of the environment to "local communities"[16] or to reduce agricultural runoff by mandating a radical change in the crop mix to favor perennials over annual crops.[17] Like the indigenous communities living in New England at the time the Pilgrims arrived, and like the Pilgrims themselves, we need to deal with the world, and our own flawed human nature, "as is."

To this end, we make three modest, but hopefully transformative, proposals.

First, we propose to reclaim the commons by recommending that the agricultural community engage with local, state, and national governmental entities in drafting a set of enforceable, regulatory initiatives aimed at limiting agriculture's impact on the environment. Obvious initial targets include reducing agricultural runoff to surface waters by requiring that all farms adopt land-use practices (such as buffers and no-till agriculture) that, similar to the current law regulating point-source polluters, represent the "best-available-control-technology" for reducing agricultural runoff. We also propose reviving the practice from the New England commons of limiting the number of animals allowed in an animal feeding operation. This limit should be set based on the characteristics of the land on which the animals are confined, and the vulnerability of potential receiving waters. Such limits would apply to the farm itself, whether or not the farm owners are producing their own output or producing for a third party as part of a contract-farming arrangement. We propose that farm use of herbicides and pesticides be limited to reflect environmental vulnerabilities peculiar to the farm site, even as limits to point-source pollution are determined by the particularities of the local air shed or receiving waters.

---

16. Ricoveri, *Nature for Sale.*

17. The Land Institute, *A 50-Year Farm Bill.* Accessed 12/30/21.

Second, we propose that the current agricultural commodity price support system be replaced by a farm income support system that assures a modest income floor to agricultural producers who produce and supply to the market their own crops, dairy, eggs, and meat. By decoupling federal farm subsidies from farm output, smaller sized farms would be spared from the competitive disadvantage they suffer under the present output-based price-support system. Replacing an output-based price-support system with a farm-income support system would diminish the ability of U.S. farm exports to compete, unfairly, with farm output in those countries unable to provide similar subsidies to their agricultural producers.

Third and finally, we propose that all of us who support the farm sector tone the rhetoric down and accept our own stewardship responsibility as both consumers and producers of agricultural output whose activities affect the health of the land, water, air, and the animals we depend on. We need to stop creating illusory demons of marketplaces, governments, and corporations, and start accepting and honoring our own responsibility for stewarding, or destroying, this world, this global commons. Like New England's agrarians, we need to recognize that stewardship of the commons requires coordination and enforcement, and we need to acknowledge that rather than vilify government, we need to employ it in service of our stewardship goals.

New England's colonial agrarians recognized that, despite living in a theocracy that required weekly church attendance and public confessions of faith, government was needed to establish and enforce limits on the use of the critical, common resources required for survival. We no longer live in a theocracy, but we are citizens of a representative democracy which we can employ to establish and enforce limits on our use of the commons, limits that we cannot rely on liberty or virtue to realize and protect. We need to restore the commons as both an achievable goal and an important constraint on our actions. Two hundred years of experience in New England demonstrates that such a goal is possible. It is time to pursue it.

# Bibliography

Adams, John. *Diary and Autobiography of John Adams: Diary 1782–1804. Autobiography, part one to October 1776.* Edited by Lyman Henry Butterfield. Cambridge: Athenænum, 1964.

Attfield, Robin. "Environmental Sensibility and Critiques of Stewardship." In *Environmental Stewardship: Critical Perspectives—Past and Present,* edited by R. J. Berry, 76–91. Edinburgh: T. & T. Clark, 2006.

———. *The Ethics of the Global Environment.* Edinburgh: Edinburgh University Press, 2015.

Bates, Samuel, ed. *Records of the Town of Braintree, 1640 to 1793.* Randolf, MA: Daniel H. Huxford, 1886.

Baxter, Richard. *Methodus Theologiæ Christianæ.* London: M. White & T. Snowden, 1681.

Bell, Michael M. "Did New England Go Downhill?" *Geographical Review* 79.4 (1989) 450–66. https://doi.org/10.2307/215118.

Berry, Wendell. "The Agrarian Standard." *Orion Magazine.* https://orionmagazine.org/article/the-agrarian-standard.

———. *Another Turn of the Crank: Essays.* Berkeley, CA: Counterpoint, 1995.

———. *The Long-Legged House.* Berkeley, CA: Counterpoint, 1969.

Bowyer, Jerry. "Lessons from a Capitalist Thanksgiving." *Forbes,* November 27, 2008. https://www.forbes.com/2008/11/27/thanksgiving-economy-history-oped-cx_jb_1127bowyer.html?sh=671d1523460a.

Bradford, William. *Bradford's History of the Plymouth Settlement, 1608–1650.* New York: Dutton and Company, 1920.

———. *Of Plymouth Plantation.* New York: Capricorn, 1962.

Brown, B. Katherine. "Freemanship in Puritan Massachusetts." *The American Historical Review* 59.4 (1954) 865–83. https://doi.org/10.2307/1845121.

# Bibliography

Buchanan, Joseph. *The Philosophy of Human Nature*. Richmond, KY: J. A. Grimes, 1812.

Bulkeley, Peter. "The Gospel Covenant." In *The Puritans in America: A Narrative Anthology*, edited by Alan Heimert and Andrew Delbanco, 117–21. Cambridge: Harvard University Press, 1985.

Callicott, J. Baird. *In Defense of the Land Ethic: Essays in Environmental Philosophy*. Albany, NY: State University of New York Press, 1989.

Cascade Policy Institute. "What Governor Bradford Learned at Plymouth's First Thanksgiving." https://cascadepolicy.org/economic-opportunity/what-governor-bradford-learned-at-plymouths-first-thanksgiving/.

Cathey, C. O. "SIDNEY WELLER: ANTE-BELLUM PROMOTER OF AGRICULTURAL REFORM." *The North Carolina Historical Review* 31.1 (1954) 1–17. http://www.jstor.org/stable/23516653.

Cato, Marcus Porcius. *Cato: On Farming—De Agricultura*. Translated by Andrew Dalby. London: Prospect, 1998.

Cicero, Marcus Tullius. *Tusculanae disputationum*. Translated by Thomas Wilson Dougan and Robert Mitchell Henry. Cambridge: Cambridge University Press, 1905.

Clark, Christopher. *The Roots of Rural Capitalism: Western Massachusetts, 1780–1860*. Ithaca, NY: Cornell University Press, 1990.

Colden, Cadwallader. *The Principles of Action in Matter*. London, 1751.

Condillac, Etienne Bonnet De. *Essay on the Origin of Human Knowledge*. Translated by Hans Aarsleff. Cambridge: Cambridge University Press, 2001.

Cooper, Thomas. *A View of the Metaphysical and Physiological Arguments in Favor of Materialism*. Philadelphia: Re-published and sold by A. Small, 1823.

Cotton, John. *An Exposition upon the Thirteenth Chapter of the Revelation by that reverend and eminent servant of the Lord, Mr. John Cotton . . . ; taken from his mouth in short-writing, and some part of it corrected by himself soon after the preaching thereof ; and all of it since viewed over by a friend to him . . . wherein some mistakes were amended, but nothing of the sense altered*. London: Thomas Allen, 1656. Reprint, Ann Arbor, MI: Text Creation Partnership, 2011. http://name.umdl.umich.edu/A34679.0001.001.

———. "God's Promise to His Plantations." In *The Puritans in America: A Narrative Anthology*, edited by Alan Heimert and Andrew Delbanco, 75–80. Cambridge: Harvard University Press, 1985.

Cudworth, Ralph. *The True Intellectual System of the Universe. The First Part: wherein all the reason and philosophy of atheism is confuted and its impossibility demonstrated*. London: Richard Royston, 1678.

Cushman, Robert. "Reasons and Considerations Touching the Lawfulness of Removing out of England into the Parts of America." In *The Puritans in America: A Narrative Anthology*, edited by Alan Heimert and Andrew Delbanco, 41–44. Cambridge: Harvard University Press, 1985.

———. "A Sermon Preached at Plimmoth in New-England December 9, 1621." In *American Sermons: The Pilgrims to Martin Luther King, Jr.*, edited by Michael Warner, 1–27. New York: Library of America, 1999.

# Bibliography

————. *The Sin and Danger of Self Love*. London, Nathaniel Coverly, 1785. Early English Books Online Text Creation Partnership, https://quod.lib. umich.edu/cgi/t/text/text-idx?c=evans;idno=N14962.0001.001.

Davenport, John. "The Saint's Anchor-Hold." In *The Puritans in America*, edited by Alan Heimert and Andrew Deblanco, 218-23. Cambridge: Harvard University Press, 1985.

Donahue, Brian. "Environmental Stewardship and Decline in Old New England." *Journal of the Early Republic* 24.2 (2004) 234-41. http://www. jstor.org/stable/4141501.

————. *The Great Meadow: Farmers and the Land in Colonial Concord*. New Haven: Yale University Press, 2004.

Dwight, Timothy. *Greenfield Hill: A Poem in Seven Parts*. New York: Printed by Childs and Swaine, 1794.

Edwards, Jonathan. "The Memoirs of Jonathan Edwards." In *Philosophy in America: From the Puritans to James*, edited by Paul Anderson and Max Fisch. New York: Appleton Century, 1939.

————. *The Works of Jonathan Edwards, D.D., late president of Union College: with a memoir of his life and character*. Boston: Doctrinal Tract and Book Society, 1850.

————. *Sinners in the Hands of an Angry God*. Boston: S. Kneeland and T. Green, 1741.

Eliot, Jared. *Essays upon Field Husbandry in New England, and Other Papers, 1748-1762*. New York: Columbia University Press, 1934.

Elliot, John. *The Grace of God Asserted to be Saving and Increated: and James Forbes proved a false witness, in affirming it to be no grace, and a great nothing*. London: Tho. Northcott, 1695.

Field, Barry, and Martha Kimball. *Managing Common-Property Resources: Agricultural Land in Colonial New England*. Indiana University Workshop in Political Theory and Policy Analysis, 1994. http://dlc.dlib.indiana.edu/ dlc/bitstream/handle/10535/8144/Managing%20Common-property%20 Resources.pdf?sequence=1&isAllowed=y,/.

Franc, Michael. "Pilgrims Beat 'Communism' with Free Market." The Heritage Foundation, November 22, 2005. https://www.heritage.org/markets-and-finance/commentary/pilgrims-beat-communism-free-market/.

Franklin, Benjamin. *The Papers of Benjamin Franklin, vol. 15, January 1 through December 31, 1768*. Edited by William B. Willcox. New Haven, CT: Yale University Press, 1972.

————. "Positions to be Examined, Concerning National Wealth." In *Essays of Benjamin Franklin*, edited by G. E. Putnam, 141-45. New York: Putnam's Sons, 1927. https://onlinebooks.library.upenn.edu/webbin/book/ lookupname?key=Franklin%2C%20Benjamin%2C%201706%2D1790.

Govan, Thomas P. "Agrarian and Agrarianism: A Study in the Use and Abuse of Words." *The Journal of Southern History* 30.1 (1964) 36-40.

Greene, Evarts, and Virginia Harrington. *American Population before the Federal Census of 1790*. New York: Columbia University Press, 1993.

# Bibliography

Harrington, James. *The Commonwealth of Oceana*. New York: Prism Key, 2012.

Heimert, Alan, and Andrew Delbanco, eds. *The Puritans in America: A Narrative Anthology*. Cambridge: Harvard University Press, 1985.

Helvétius, Claude Adrien. *De L'esprit*. London: Mr. Dudley and Co., 1759.

Henretta, James A. "Families and Farms: Mentalité in Pre-Industrial America." *The William and Mary Quarterly*, Third Series, 35.1 (1978) 3–32.

Hightower, James. *Hard Tomatoes, Hard Times: A Report of the Agribusiness Accountability Project on the Failure of America's Land Grant College Complex*. Agriculture Accountability Project. Cambridge, MA: Schenkman, 1972.

Holbach, Paul Henri Thiry, baron d'. *The System of Nature*. Manchester, UK: Clinamen, 1999.

Hooker, Thomas. *The Danger of Desertion*. London: Printed by G. M. for George Edwards, 1641.

———. *The Soul's Preparation for Christ*. London: Printed by J. G. for R. Dawlman, 1658.

Horace. *Odes and Epodes*. Edited by Michele Lowrie. Oxford: Oxford University Press, 2009.

Hurt, Douglas. *American Agriculture: A Brief History*. West Lafayette, IN: Purdue University Press, 2020.

Jackson, Wes. *Call for a Revolution in Agriculture*. Edited by Hildegarde Hannum. Mount Holyoke College, MA: Center for New Economics, 1981.

———. *Consulting the Genius of the Place*. Berkeley: Counterpoint, 2010.

Jackson, Wes, and Wendell Berry. *A Conversation between Wendell Berry and Wes Jackson*. Edited by Hildegarde Hannum. Great Barrington, MA: Center for New Economics, 2016.

Jefferson, Thomas. *The Complete Jefferson*. Edited by Saul K. Padover. New York: Tudor, 1943.

———. *Notes on the State of Virginia*. Public Broadcasting Service. https://www.pbs.org/wgbh/aia/part3/3h490t.html.

Johnson, Edward. *Wonder-Working Providence of Sions Savior in New England*. Andover, MA: W. F. Draper, 1867.

Johnson, Samuel. *Elements Philosophica*. London: A. Millar, 1754.

———. *An Introduction to the Study of Philosophy*. New London, CT: Printed by T. Green, 1743.

———. "Letter to George Berkeley." In *Philosophy in America: From the Puritans to James*, edited by Paul Anderson and Max Fisch, 58–60. New York: Appleton Century, 1939.

Jones, Alice Hanson. "Wealth Estimates for the New England Colonies about 1770." *The Journal of Economic History* 32.1 (1972) 98–127. http://www.jstor.org/stable/2117179.

———. "Wealth and Growth of the Thirteen Colonies: Some Implications." *The Journal of Economic History* 44.2 (1984) 239–54. http://www.jstor.org/stable/2120701.

# Bibliography

Kirshenmann, Frederick. *Cultivating an Ecological Conscience: Essays from a Farmer Philosopher*. Louisville, KY: University Press of Kentucky, 2010.

The Land Institute. *A 50-Year Farm Bill*. 2009. https://landinstitute.org/wp-content/uploads/2016/09/FB-edited-7-6-10.pdf.

Libby, Edgar Howard. "Early History of the Fence." *The American Garden* IX.11 (1888) 401–2.

Lindert, Peter H., and Jeffery G. Williamson. "American Colonial Incomes, 1650 to 1774." NBER Working Paper Series, 2014. https://www.nber.org/papers/w19861.

Locke, John. *Two Treatises of Government and a Letter Concerning Toleration*. Edited by Ian Shapiro. New Haven, CT: Yale University Press, 2003.

Mather, Cotton. *The Christian Philosopher*. Edited by Winton Solberg. Champaign, IL: University of Illinois Press, 1994.

———. *The Christian Philosopher*. Charlestown, MA: The Middlesex Bookstore, 1720.

Mather, Increase. *An Essay for the Recording of Illustrious Providences*. Boston: Printed by Samuel Green for Joseph Browning, 1684.

Malthus, T. R. "An Essay on the Principle of Population." *The Critical Review*. London: J. Johnson, 1804.

Mayer, Frederick. *A History of American Thought*. Dubuque, IO: Brown, 1951.

MacLear, Anne B. *Early New England Towns: A Comparative Study of Their Development*. New York: Columbia University Press, 1908.

*Massachusetts Body of Liberties (1641)*. Hanover Historical Texts Project. Retrieved September 25, 2021. https://history.hanover.edu/texts/masslib.html.

Miller, Perry. *The New England Mind: The Seventeenth Century*. Cambridge: Harvard University Press, 1939.

More, Henry. *A Collection of Several Philosophical Writings, 1662*. New York: Garland, 1978.

Mourt, G. *Relation*. London: Printed by J. Dawson for John Bellamie, 1622.

Nash, Roderick. *The Rights of Nature: A History of Environmental Ethics*. Madison, WI: University of Wisconsin Press, 1989.

Nobles, Gregory. "The Rise of Merchants in Rural Market Towns: A Case Study of Eighteenth-Century Northampton, Massachusetts." *Journal of Social History* 24.1 (1990) 5–23. http://www.jstor.org/stable/3787628.

Olmstead, Gracy. "Wendell Berry's Right Kind of Farming." *The New York Times*, October 1, 2018. https://www.nytimes.com/2018/10/01/opinion/wendell-berry-agriculture-farm-bill.html.

Ostrom, Elinor. *Governing the Commons: The Evolution of Institutions for Collective Action*. Cambridge: Cambridge University Press, 1990.

Paine, Thomas. "Agrarian Justice." In *Collected Writings*, edited by Eric Foner, 399–400. New York: Library of America, 1995.

Plato. *The Republic of Plato*. Translated by Benjamin Jowett. Oxford: Oxford University Press, 1888.

# Bibliography

Powell, Sumner. *Puritan Village*. Middleton, CT: Wesleyan University Press, 1963.

Priestly, Joseph. *Institutes of Natural and Revealed Religion*. London: Joseph Johnson, 1772.

Pruitt, Bettye Hobbs. "Self-Sufficiency and the Agricultural Economy of Eighteenth-Century Massachusetts." *The William and Mary Quarterly* 41.3 (1984) 334–64. https://doi.org/10.2307/1922729.

Quesnay, François. "General Maxims of the Economical Government in an Agricultural Kingdom." In *The Library of Original Sources*. New York: University Press of the Pacific, 1907. https://www.marxists.org/reference/subject/economics/quesnay/1767/maxims.htm.

Rasmussen, Larry. *Earth Honoring Faith*. Oxford: Oxford University Press, 2015.

Rawls, John. *A Theory of Justice*. Oxford: Oxford University Press, 1999.

Reid, Thomas. *An Inquiry into the Human Mind on the Principles of Common Sense*. Edinburgh: Edinburgh University Press, 2000.

Ricoveri, Giovanna. *Nature for Sale: The Commons Versus Commodities*. New York: Pluto, 2014.

Rolston, Holmes. *Environmental Ethics: Duties to and Values in the Natural World*. Philadelphia: Temple University Press, 1988.

Rush, Benjamin. *An Oration, delivered before the American Philosophical Society, held in Philadelphia on the 27th of February, 1786: containing an enquiry into the influence of physical causes upon the moral faculty*. Philadelphia: Printed by Charles Cist, 1786.

Ryle, Gilbert. *The Concept of Mind*. New York: Barnes & Noble, 1959.

Schneider, Herbert Wallace. *A History of American Philosophy*. New York: Columbia University Press, 1947.

Seneca, Lucius Annaeus. *Twenty and Two Epistles of Lucius Annaeus Seneca, the Philosopher*. London: Printed for Thomas Harper, 1654.

Steward, Dugald. *Elements of the Philosophy of the Human Mind*. London: Printed for T. Cadell and W. Davies, 1808.

Saint Olaf College. *Wendell Berry House*. SustainAbilities. Retrieved September 25, 2021. https://sustainabilities.stolaf.edu/wendell-berry-house/.

Smith, Daniel Scott, and Michael S. Hindus. "Premarital Pregnancy in America 1640–1971: An Overview and Interpretation." *The Journal of Interdisciplinary History* 5.4 (1975) 537–70.

Steven Stoll. *Larding the Lean Earth: Soil and Society in Nineteenth Century America*. New York: Hill & Wang, 2002.

Szatmary, David P. *Shays' Rebellion: The Making of an Agrarian Insurrection*. Amherst, MA, University of Massachusetts Press, 1980.

Tannenbaum, Jerrold. "Animals and the Law: Property, Cruelty, Rights." *Social Research* 62.3 (1995) 539–607. http://www.jstor.org/stable/40971109.

Taylor, John. *Arator: Being a Series of Agricultural Essays, Practical and Political*. Edited by M. E. Bradford. Indianapolis: Liberty Classics, 1977.

Taylor, Paul W. *Respect for Nature: A Theory of Environmental Ethics*. Princeton, NJ: Princeton University Press, 1986.

# Bibliography

Thomas, Isaiah, and Ebenezar T. Andrews. *The Perpetual Laws of the Commonwealth of Massachusetts from the Establishment of Its Constitution in the Year 1780 to the End of the Year 1800, vol. 1.* Boston: 1801. https://www.google.co.uk/books/edition/The_Perpetual_Laws_of_ the_Commonwealth_o/ADw4AAAAIAAJ?hl=en&gbpv=0.

Thompson, Paul B. *The Agrarian Vision: Sustainability and Environmental Ethics.* Lexington, KY: The University of Kentucky Press, 2010.

————. *The Spirit of the Soil: Agriculture and Environmental Ethics.* London: Routledge, 1995.

Thoreau, Henry David. *Journal XII, March 2, 1859–November 30, 1859.* Edited by Bradford Torrey. Boston: Houghton Mifflin, 1906.

————. *Walden: A Fully Annotated Edition.* Edited by Jeffrey S. Cramer. New Haven, CT: Yale University Press, 2004.

Townsend, Harvey Gates. *Philosophical Idea in the United States.* New York: American Book Co., 1934.

Tracy, Patricia J. "Re-Considering Migration within Colonial New England." *Journal of Social History* 23.1 (1989) 93–113. http://www.jstor.org/ stable/3787566.

Turner, R. E. "Declining Bacteria, Lead, and Sulphate, and Rising pH and Oxygen in the Lower Mississippi River." *Ambio* 50 (2021) 1731–38. https://doi.org/10.1007/s13280-20-01499-92.

Twelve Southerners. *I'll Take My Stand: The South and the Agrarian Tradition.* 75th Anniversary ed. With a new introduction by Susan V. Donaldson. Baton Rouge: Louisiana State University Press, 2006.

Valls, Andrew. "Locke, Slavery, and the Two Treatises." In *Race and Racism in Modern Philosophy*, 89–107. Ithaca, NY: Cornell University Press, 2005.

Virgil. *The Georgics.* Translated by John Dryden. New York: Heritage, 1953.

Walcott, Robert R. "Husbandry in Colonial New England." *The New England Quarterly* 9.2 (1936) 218–52. https://doi.org/10.2307/360390.

White, Lynn. *The Historical Roots of our Ecological Crisis.* Washington, DC: Science, 1967.

Winthrop, John. "A Declaration in Defense of an Order of Court in May 1637." In *The Puritans in America: A Narrative Anthology*, edited by Alan Heimert and Andrew Delbanco, 164–67. Cambridge: Harvard University Press, 1985.

————. "A Model of Christian Charity." In *The Puritans in America: A Narrative Anthology*, edited by Alan Heimert and Andrew Delbanco, 81–92. Cambridge: Harvard University Press, 1985.

————. "Reasons to Be Considered for Justifying the Intended Plantation in New England and for Encouraging Such Whose Hearts God Shall Move to Join with Them in It." In *The Puritans in America: A Narrative Anthology*, edited by Alan Heimert and Andrew Delbanco, 70–74. Cambridge: Harvard University Press, 1985.

————. *Winthrop's Journal, "History of New England," 1630–49.* New York: Scribner's Sons, 1908.

Wolterstorff, Nicholas. *Reason within the Bounds of Religion.* Grand Rapids, MI: Wm. B. Eerdmans Publishing, 1984.

World Monuments Fund. "Cultural Landscape of Hadley, Massachusetts." July, 2017. https://www.wmf.org/project/cultural-landscape-hadley-massachusetts.

Zernike, Kate. "The Pilgrims Were . . . Socialists?" *The New York Times,* November 20, 2010. https://www.nytimes.com/2010/11/21/weekinreview/21zernike.html.

# Index

animal feedlots, 62, 66
animal protection, 61
anti-industrial agrarian impulse, of
	the Twelve Southerners, 56
Aristotle, x
art, of farming, 29
"as much and as good" criterion, 61
Attfield, Robin, xiii

Bass, Jonathan, 43, 43n2
Baxter, Richard, 11
Berkeley, George, 19–20
Berry, Wendell, xiii, xiv, 55–56, 63
"best-available-control-technology,"
	66
biblical narratives and teaching, of
	the European Reformation, 5
body and law, regulating use of the
	commons, 40
The Body of Liberties, 1, 51
bonds of love, extending to the
	community, 10
Bonnot de Condillac, Etienne, 19
Bowyer, Jerry, 44
Bradford, William, 13, 35, 45
Braintree, Massachusetts, 36, 42–43
Brattle, Thomas, 17
brotherly affection, bonds of, 10
Buchanan, Joseph, 18–19
Bulkeley, Peter, 11, 13
bureaucracy, needed for the
	commons, 40

Cambridge Platonists, in the
	colonies, 29
cash-based economy, 48
causal relations, existing through
	the greater power of God, 24
"chain of debt," leading to Shays'
	Rebellion, 48
Charles I, 3
The Christian Philosopher (Mather),
	23
Christian theism, 5, 22, 29, 30

Christianity, of Thomas Jefferson, xiii
Church of England, 3
civic ethics, issues in, 55
civil right, to the earth, 7
Clark, Christopher, 47
Clean Air and Clean Water Acts,
	results of, 63n12
Colden, Cadwallader, 17, 22
colonial colleges, emphasis on
	science, 17
colonial hunters, directly accessing
	bounties, 15
colonial New England, agrarian
	tradition, xvi
colonial theology, on land and labor,
	2–16
colonies, viewing *sub specie
	aeternitatis*, 13
colonists
	appealed to divine ownership, 6
	giving primacy to physical
		bodies, 17
	gradually acquired other skills
		to earn a living, 48
	guiding to establish a society
		dedicated to God, 13
	sought a just government, 4
common fields, 34, 35
common good
	erosion in the commitment to, 41
	farming oriented in New
		England to, 2
	Locke appealed to, 8
	managing critical resources
		for, 60
	theological support for stress
		on, 12
common grazing land, 36
common ground, in a variety of
	philosophical traditions, 31
common lands, joint ownership and
	management control of, 50
commoners, 47, 54

# Index

the commons
  abandoned, 46
  boundaries of allowed no more
    than one share, 47
  employing a representative
    democracy, 67
  establishing, 6
  existed as an institution, 33
  for just distribution of goods
    and care for the poor and
    children, 4
  maintaining, xvi
  in New England agrarianism,
    xvi, 32–41
  overuse of, 64
  persistent emphasis on, 2
  physical boundaries of, 49
  providing a subsistence standard
    of living, 52
  restoring, xv
  as a sustainable way of farming,
    57
  theological basis for, 12
  threats to colonial New
    England's, 42–57
  as a way to live within means, 54
commons-based agrarian system,
    produced enduring results,
    52
*The Commonwealth of Oceana*
  (Harrington), x
communism, New England
    commons and, 33
communitarian-based agrarianism,
    demise of, xvi
communitarianism, shift to
    individualism, 55
community
  demonstrating love of neighbor,
    4–5, 9
  as described by Berry, xiv
  as members of the same body,
    10
  shaped by the commons, 53
  traits of, 35

conflicts, sparked by religious fervor
  of, 15–16
constraints, on individual freedom,
  13
Cooper, Thomas, 18
cosmic optimism, as the final
  Puritan disposition, 15
cosmos, dependence upon God, 5
cottage-level manufacturing activity,
  increase in, 48
Cotton, John, 6, 64
country store, no longer accepting
  farm produce, 48
covenantal life, successes of, 11
creation, philosophy of, 5
creation and regeneration, theology
  of, 9
credit and debt, complex webs of,
  39–40
critical resources, managing for the
  common good, 35, 60
Cromwell, 3
Cudworth, Ralph, 29
cultivation, 7, 8
Cushman, Robert, 10, 13, 33

*The Danger of Desertion* (Hooker), 4
Davenport, John, 4
Davison, Donald, xin4
Delbanco, Andrew, 25, 28
dependence, of the cosmos upon
  God, 5
d'Holbach, Baron, 19, 22
divine beauty, exaltation of, 15
divine ownership, 9
Donahue, Brian, 38, 54
dualism, ethical problem of, 25
Dwight, Timothy, 11, 30

earth, double right to, 7
Earth is the Lord's, and the fullness
  thereof, 6
economic gain, pivotal in early
  American life, 28

economic thought, physiocratic
school of, 26
economic welfare, in terms of a
greater divine economy,
10–11
economies of scale, in reference to
Concord's Great Field, 38
Edwards, Jonathan, 14, 19, 21
*Elementa Philosophica* (Johnson), 24
Elijah, 29
Eliot, Jared, 30
Eliot, John, 11
encroachments, to the commons, 37
England, New England mounting
trade deficit with, 48
environmental degradation,
agriculture's contributions
to, 62
environmentalists, schism with
farmers, xv
*An Essay for the Recording of
Illustrious Providences*
(Mather), 13
*Essays on Field Husbandry* (Eliot), 30
ethical agrarianism, practitioners
of, xv
European agricultural practices,
translated poorly to North
America, 3
exclusionary principle, 50, 51
*Exposition on the Thirteenth Chapter
of Revelation* (Cotton), 64
external constrains, in the Puritan
model, 12

farm income support system, 67
farmers
blaming government for the
wretched state of, xiii
inclined toward virtue, 12
of New England left estates with
less material wealth, 39
preferring a "moral economy," 2
romantic view of yeoman, xin4

trusting reason because it
originated with God, 29
value of in a democratic culture,
xi
"Farmer's Letter" (Dickinson), 30
farming
avoiding endorsing government
regulation of, xiii
mind of God and, 28–31
moving to less settled areas, 52
New England and the South as
divergent, 53
not always praised as a vital,
virtuous practice, ix
oriented in New England to the
common good, 2
praising traced back to Greco-
Roman times, x
smaller percentage of inhabitants
able to pursue, 48
farmlands, per-acre yield in New
England, 52
farms, sparing smaller sized, 67
"fashion of hogs," natural-policy
behavior as, 10
Father-Son-Holy Spirit relationship,
calling humanity to a wider
fellowship, 21
federal farm subsidies, decoupling
from farm output, 67
Fletcher, John Gould, xin4
"food democracy," advocating, xi
"founding fathers," of communities,
37
Franc, Michael, 44
Franklin, Benjamin, 22, 26–27
free market economy, 55

Galileo, 17
God
divided the land of Canaan by
lots, x
giving land to those whom He
chooses, 6

# Index

# Index

www.ingramcontent.com/pod-product-compliance
Lightning Source LLC
Chambersburg PA
CBHW030849090426
42737CB00009B/1162